The Scripts Parents Write
and
the Roles Babies Play

The Scripts Parents Write and the Roles Babies Play

The Importance of Being Baby

BERTRAND G. CRAMER, M.D.

Translated from the French by Gillian Gill

JASON ARONSON INC.
Northvale, New Jersey
London

THE MASTER WORK SERIES

1997 softcover edition

This work was first published in France by Editions Calmann-Lévy under the title *Profession Bébé*, © 1989 by Calmann-Lévy. Original English translation titled *The Importance of Being Baby*, © 1992 by Addison-Wesley Publishing Company. Interior photos by Steven Trefonides.

Library of Congress Cataloging-in-Publication Data

Cramer, Bertrand G.
    [Profession bébé. English]
    The scripts parents write and the roles babies play : the
importance of being baby / Bertrand G. Cramer.
        p. cm. — (The master work series)
    Originally published: The importance of being baby. Reading, Mass. :
Addison-Wesley Pub. Co., c1992.
    Includes bibliographical references and index.
    ISBN 0–7657–0136–7 (alk. paper)
    1. Infants—Development. 2. Infant psychology. 3. Parent and
child. I. Cramer, Bertrand G. Importance of being baby.
II. Title. III. Series.
HQ774.C73313   1997
305.231—dc21   97–35914

Printed in the United States of America on acid-free paper. For information and catalog write to Jason Aronson Inc., 230 Livingston Street, Northvale, New Jersey 07647-1731. Or visit our website: http://www.aronson.com

Contents

Contents
❦

Introduction

*I*nfant psychiatry, the optimistic field in which I have been practicing for many years, is poorly named. The "patient" is not a lone baby perched on a couch but is at least two people—mother and infant—or sometimes three, including the father. As the pediatrician and psychoanalyst D.W. Winnicott pointed out: "If you show me a baby, you certainly show me also someone caring for a baby, or at least a pram with someone's eyes and ears glued to it" (Winnicott 1964, 1986). The origins of infant psychiatry can be found in the nineteen-forties, when René Spitz and others observed what happened to babies deprived of mothering. They develop a series of symptoms that range from failure to thrive to repeated infections and even to a state that resembles depression. At around the same time, childhood autism was discovered; it became evident that even very young children (less than 2 years old) could demonstrate bona fide psychiatric symptoms in the form of social avoidance, bizarre behaviors, and oddities of thought.

Psychoanalysis, looking only at adults, had long postulated that psychic problems have their origin in early childhood. Researchers and clinicians sought to find these early signs of psychiatric imbalance in children, and then in infants. Margaret Mahler described how an infant's problems are enmeshed in the mother-infant relationship. A main task of human development, she maintained, is to achieve a balance between the baby's need to remain dependent on his mother and the necessity for increasing autonomy in order to achieve a process of individuation.

As specialists studied mothers and babies more closely, they identified many subtle forms of disorder in mother-infant relationships. It became clear that psychological problems could be found even in very young infants, that infancy was probably an ideal time to practice prevention of certain psychiatric disorders, and that when infants show various symptoms, psychotherapy with parents and babies could achieve very satisfactory results.

For anyone who cares about children, infant psychiatry, or mother-infant psychotherapy, holds several promises. First, as we will show in this book, it can bring relief to very anxious parents whose infants suffer from many kinds of symptoms: sleeping and eating difficulties, behavior problems, and—especially—disturbed relationships. Such therapy can bring *fast* relief and this is essential: parents suffer greatly when the baby they had so eagerly expected turns out to be a source of worry or—worse—arouses feelings of hatred. They are very much relieved when they are enabled to renew a pleasurable link to their infant. The growing field of early intervention puts great emphasis on strengthening the bond between parents and young infants, because so many factors can weaken and threaten this relationship. There are now quite a few methods used to achieve this aim. Mother-infant psychotherapy is but one of them. Among its advantages is the way it allows parents to re-work old conflicts and anxieties that might otherwise have remained unresolved.

Mother-infant psychotherapy also offers the possibility of preventing such symptoms and troubled relationships. If we can intervene before disturbed patterns between parents and children become fixed, we will have more of a chance to avoid self-perpetuating problems. Experience precludes my believing that prevention in psychiatry has the same remarkable impact as, for example, vaccinations have in preventing infectious diseases. But it is certain that these early forms of psychotherapy, practiced in infancy, achieve quicker and more dramatic results than when therapy is practiced at a later age.

Finally, the insights drawn from infant psychiatry have value for all parents. While the stories that follow come from my practice as a psychiatrist, the problems in them, unlike many of the cases seen in adult psychiatry, are not exceptional. They concern fears, expectations, and doubts that *all* parents experience—in more or less intense form—as their relationship with their children gradually unfolds.

We all feel, at one point or another, pangs of anxiety about the future of our children, about their abilities and their chances in life. At the same time, we all have doubts about our abilities as care-givers and educators. Parent-child relationships are a continuous drama; periods of tranquillity follow scenes of fear or sadness. During early infancy and the first two years, passions can be most intense. While a baby who corresponds to our ideals brings a tremendous boost to our self-esteem, an infant who is difficult to gratify, or who has a sickness, or who wakes up every night, can bring havoc into the most sturdy families.

My hope is that parents will recognize themselves in these stories of those who have decided to consult me and will be heartened to realize that many of these painful situations can be unravelled, understood, and— eventually—overcome. Understanding what goes on in the first months between parents and infants is not only fascinating but it might also be the beginning of wisdom in the "impossible" task of raising a child.

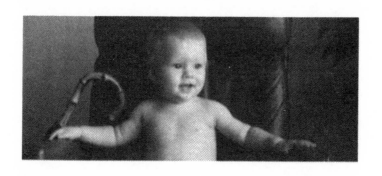

New Actors in Old Scripts

A pediatrician colleague asks
if he can refer a patient to me, little Marie Martin, thirteen months old. My colleague has become concerned
because Mrs. Evelyn Martin, Marie's young mother,
says she is unable to cope with her child's shrieking and
crying.

I am surprised to discover just how distressed the
mother is, how deeply upset by her baby's behavior.
Sometimes, for no apparent reason, she tells me, Marie
goes into a tantrum and hits and scratches her.

When I see the two together I have trouble believing that a fully grown woman should feel threatened by
such a passive and innocent-looking little child. All the
same, violence is in the air. As soon as Marie puts her
hand close to her mother's face, Mrs. Martin jerks away
and says, "Don't scratch me!"

What a bizarre response! How can Evelyn read
violent intentions into such an innocuous gesture? As I

watch this distraught mother and passive child, I see that life for Evelyn and her daughter has already turned into a drama of misunderstanding. The idyllic relationship that usually develops between a mother and her baby has already broken down at a very early stage.

Why does Evelyn read violence into a gesture that could well be a caress? How has she come to fear the child she had once desired so intensely? And what does this mean for Marie? How does she experience the fear, her mother's frightened assumption that she means to hurt her?

Is it possible that Marie has already noticed that her mother is unable to bear even a hint of roughness and that her passivity is already an attempt to adapt to her mother's extreme sensitivity? Is it possible that Marie has already understood that, if she is too lively, her mother will shy away? Does she sense that she can be perceived as a dangerous enemy?

As we continue our sessions, I realize that Evelyn and Marie have reached an impasse. They live in an atmosphere of crisis and Evelyn is already prophesying a disaster. The apparent irremediability of the situation makes her deeply anxious. What will happen if this misunderstanding persists, drawing mother and daughter into a state of armed warfare?

The situation Evelyn and Marie find themselves in is far from unusual. Many people discover, to their sorrow, that misunderstandings arise to spoil the parent-child relationship, sometimes from the time the child is born. In this book I shall explore the hidden causes that set such conflicts in motion, constantly referring back to the case of Marie and Evelyn as my basic point of reference. I shall try to explain how Marie used passivity to adapt to her mother's fears of violence, and why Evelyn was gripped with such anxiety every time her daughter touched her.

The fate of a human being may be decided in the first months of life. Nonetheless, one reason for writing this book is to make clear that fate is not fixed and immutable, that help can be found. We shall follow the story of Evelyn and Marie and seek to uncover the causes of their misunderstanding. As we do so, we shall analyze the mysterious chemistry that binds parents and children together for better and, sometimes, for worse.

The Dream Child Comes to Earth

There is something about a birth that sets off the most astonishing reactions. Sometimes the baby is seen as a savior who gives a new lease on life to the parents' wounded ambitions, or who promises the perfect love of which father and mother had always dreamed. Sometimes the baby is seen as an ideal person who makes up for all the mistakes of the past, or as that other self, the partner in a complicity that needs no words.

But babies can also bring disillusion. Some are

seen as the doubles of the selves that we despise. Others are the reincarnations of hated parents. Still others, by being plain or sickly or the wrong sex, carry in their flesh the mark of our faults or failures.

Babies can arouse passionate love. They can just as easily provoke worry or even hate. My work as a psychiatrist is played out against the backdrop of the stormy passions that babies unleash. In this book I will try to show how a love relationship can become a war, how the match between a dream child and a flesh-and-blood baby can lead to a nightmare or a honeymoon.

Parents as Casting Directors

A parent's very first words about a baby can tell us what costume is being used to dress this still-naked child, what character clues are being laid, what charges are being leveled. For an astonishing phenomenon occurs when a child is born: Just as nature abhors a vacuum, so the human psyche abhors anything devoid of meaning. Faced with the unknown in the shape of their tiny new baby, parents hurry to supply an identity and a whole range of characteristics. He is handsome, strong, self-centered, rough, and, they usually add, "just like his grandfather [uncle, father, etc.]." The character traits attributed to the baby are always seen as hereditary.

This is how continuities between the generations are established and family traditions are kept going.

This is also how parents establish a rapport with the newcomer. Meeting the baby on that first day of life is an unparalleled event in human experience. In the space of a few moments parents have to take a stranger to their bosoms—for life! Now the unknown, like the void, always gives rise to anxiety. When parents attribute a set of characteristics and likenesses to their offspring, they fill the void. The strange is transformed into the familiar when it is endowed with family characteristics.

The baby, in his or her nakedness, is seen (erroneously, as we shall see later) as a blank slate. This gives rise to a whole range of psychological attributions. The baby is immediately assumed to have intentions and preferences. The process of projection (in which we exteriorize the images we carry of our own parents or of ourselves) goes on throughout our lives, but it occurs in an extraordinarily intense form at the time of birth. Quite unexpected encounters take place, as when parents manage to confuse their son with his grandfather. Imagine what a shock this can be if the grandfather was hated or feared! Far from corresponding to the ideal, the baby may suddenly seem like a ghost, taking on the disquieting shape of someone you loved or hated in the past and who now comes back to haunt you.

This is only the beginning. Having made these attributions, parents now expect their baby to follow the proper script. By the way he behaves, by the signs he gives, the baby is expected to prove that he is rightly considered to be the reincarnation of his grandfather.

All mother-child interactions form a kind of drama in which, without knowing it, the partners act out a script or scenario. I like the notion of a script because it conveys the faithful way the protagonists play out the parts laid down for them by events in the past. It is as if parents and babies are actors in a play that has already been written. Tirelessly, and with little improvisation, they rehearse scenes that take charge of their lives. These scenes correspond to unconscious fantasies and are structured by them.

Babies have their work cut out for them. Their "job" is to measure up to these parental expectations, to fit the parts in which they have been cast while at the same time fulfilling their own goals and needs. As we shall see, this is a demanding role and requires not only talent but also good training.

New Parts for Parents

Life holds certain watershed experiences that enforce change. Puberty, marriage, loss, and menopause are among these essential experiences. So also is the birth of a child.

It is easy to underestimate the revolution brought about by a birth, especially the birth of the first child. The coming of this new being mandates a simultaneous change in status; a child becomes a parent, a twosome changes into a threesome. Life will never be the same again. Confronted with these intimate revolutions in our lives, we parents have to improvise, come up with something new.

But if the alien grain of sand introduced into the system is to be sweated into a pearl, models are needed. Faced with this new life, parents will survive according to their ability to assimilate the new with the old, the eruption of difference into the familiar routine. As we invent new roles as parents, we make use of materials gathered as children. Each of us will discover the baby by means of the childhood memories that we harbor deep within. We show our readiness to raise children when the behavior of our parents to us as children becomes our own.

Suddenly, and without quite realizing it, new parents feel as if their own parents or some aspect of a parent has taken them over. They are surprised to see themselves acting in strange ways and find themselves making quite alien remarks. All this because, willy-nilly, just by the fact of becoming new parents, they turn out to be the carriers of traits inherited from their own parents. Such developments are welcome when they assist a parent to cope with his or her new role but alarming when they bring a sense of alienation or of identification with the worst faults of the parents of yesteryear.

It is within the context of this unique meeting of the impromptu and the familiar, this mixture of creativity and repetition, that we can find the connections in the way parents act and infants react.

Infant Psychiatry

It has been recognized for some time that psychological problems can afflict even very young babies. From the first days of life, they may refuse to nurse, avoid eye contact, throw up their food, or appear tense and agitated. These "symptoms" are signs of psychological anxiety, but this anxiety in the baby can be understood only when issues troubling the mother are addressed. The types of symptoms I have just listed—and many others that we shall illustrate in the course of this book—are the subject of infant psychiatry.

In my work with parents and babies, I often think of myself as a ferryman, making it possible to cross from one stage of life to another. The first crossing is from before to after birth. Parents must absorb the shock of the difference between the ideal baby of a parent's dreams and the more prosaic baby offered in reality.

When troubled parents and babies like Evelyn and
Marie come for help, I take a journey with them into the
past. Parents often do not realize that the misunderstanding occasioned by the baby has its roots in their own
childhoods. Thus it becomes essential to bring back to life
the people whom the parents are really addressing when
they make demands upon their babies. To do this, I have
to help parents let old forgotten, repressed, unconscious
anxieties and complaints well up again, just as I do with
my psychoanalytic patients. I try to link everything I'm
told about the baby back to childhood fantasies, memories, and conflicts. These had remained latent until the
entrance of a new child brought them back to life. Eventually it becomes clear which ghosts have taken possession
of the baby's cradle and how to chase them away.

My job is also to act as go-between, a sort of mes-
senger between parents and infant. I often find it necessary to translate the baby's behavior patterns, showing
that what the parent sees as tyranny or armed warfare
is only a cry for affection, a longing to be touched.
Similarly, it may be important to show the child (who
understands far more than we think) that when his or
her mother draws away it is not because of indifference
but because she seeks a clearer mark of affection.

Thus I deal with both partners (all three when the
father is present), whispering from the wings to explain
a misunderstanding here, a conflict there, hoping that
someone will take the cue.

Unlike the psychoanalytic or psychotherapeutic treatment of an adult, sessions with mothers and babies involve a great deal of action and interaction. Exchanges take place between the two and then the baby will embark on a game that I can interpret. Furthermore, my presence itself influences what occurs and provides material for commentary. I may be viewed as one of the mother's parents, or as an interloper who disturbs the intimacy of the mother-child relationship. If the father is not present, I may be viewed as the paternal third party. In other words, the mother and the child will operate a "transference" on me, giving me a role to act out just as in any other session with a therapist.

My working hypothesis is that each sequence of interactions that I observe between mother and child is a message with a meaning. Often the way they act with one another bears out what the mother has said, and thus takes on the same revelatory value as the verbal associations of the mother's words. When I am able to interpret the scenario, this often comes as a revelation to the mother. She then recognizes how a fantastic script has been shaping her daily handling of her baby and contributing to the baby's own symptoms.

When I videotape the sessions and play them back for the parents, they are often amazed by the way certain scenes are repeated and they come to understand that these scenes have roots in the past.

A Fresh Start

As we will see in Chapter 3, babies are not passive, faceless actors, ready to be molded into a ready-made role. When I can demonstrate this to parents, and show them the disparities between their unconscious scripts and the baby's individual needs, they often meet the baby for the first time. Very often this leads to a fresh start, a series of modifications that allow parents and child to begin their relationship again. Anxiety lifts, symptoms disappear.

While our children are cast from birth into roles written long ago, the scripts are not immutable. An understanding of their family roots and of the individual talents of the newborn actors will give us freedom to change the plot, to make new choices.

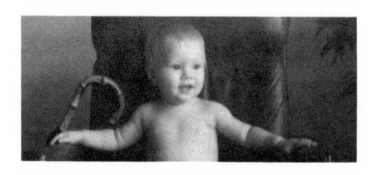

TWO

ॐ

The Red Thread

❦

*W*hen a mother calls me, she always begins with either a complaint or a worry.

In most cases, a mother complains because her child cries or howls, sleeps badly, or has a poor appetite. Sometimes, however, the situation is more complex and more upsetting: the mother may say that the baby is not affectionate enough, is selfish, or makes excessive demands on her. She may even, as we saw with Evelyn, say that the baby is rough and wants to hurt her.

At first sight it would seem unlikely that an adult woman would expect marks of affection from a baby only a few months old or that a baby could seem violent to her. And yet mothers who complain in this way are not faking. They are quite convinced of speaking the truth and sometimes they set out to demonstrate that the behavior that disturbs them is real. "See how Marie scratches me," Mrs. Martin would say to me. I give my full attention to this complaint, to the exact way it is expressed, to the emotion that accompanies it. The authenticity of the mother's *feelings* are not in doubt even if they prove to be exaggerated and out of proportion.

The nature of the complaint will pinpoint the emergence of deeper psychic pain. It is one end of the "red thread" that will lead back to another scene played out in the past. This scene will help explain the strength of the mother's reactions today.

The mother's complaints about the baby, like the theme in an opera overture, will recur again and again as the drama unfolds. This leitmotif will focus my attention, sharpen my questions, direct my curiosity. Each modulation in the theme will be vital as we move ahead in the story. My goal is to help the mother understand whom or what she is really complaining about.

My Daughter Hurts Me

Let's go back to Mrs. Martin's problems with her daughter. If we carefully decode what she says, word by word, we can uncover a whole series of clues. It's like the beginning of a treasure hunt.

Imagine the scene. Marie's mother, referred by her pediatrician, comes to see a psychiatrist she doesn't know. The meeting takes place in an interview room where two cameras, monitored from an adjacent room, record all events. Mrs. Martin has agreed to being taped, and one of the most surprising things in this type of session is that, despite the unusual setup, there is no difficulty in establishing an atmosphere of intimacy in which highly charged emotional information can be communicated. Mrs. Martin is to discover for the first time what this emotion is about.

Let us follow in detail the first ten minutes of our conversation. The mother does most of the talking. The child is on her lap. I listen, watch, and do whatever is necessary to keep this curious conversation going.

Evelyn Martin begins in this way. "Marie follows me everywhere. She has gotten very aggressive, though I don't understand why."

Then comes the description of a family dinner at a restaurant which embarrassed Evelyn deeply. Marie had suddenly started to screech, howl, drum her feet, "though I can't think why." Every effort was made to calm the child: the parents were embarrassed, the waiters annoyed. Suddenly the screaming stopped, "why I don't know."

Mrs. Martin comments: "She just gets like that, screaming louder and louder, and no one knows why."

When the Baby Is a Mystery

This description has lasted three minutes and thirty seconds. The mother seems fairly calm; on the other hand, what strikes me is how overwhelmed she says she was by her baby's behavior. She repeats four times that she does not understand the reason for this behavior; she is puzzled and upset. Marie's actions are a mystery that Evelyn cannot fathom.

When parents are unable to understand their baby's behavior and motivation, they get very anxious. They feel lost and without points of reference; they look at their infant as if he or she were a stranger. "He's like a being from outer space," one mother remarked to me about her baby.

This strangeness can be very unsettling; parents can't see themselves in this little creature they themselves have produced. Of course, the absence of language makes it harder to decode the baby's behavior, but there can be another dimension to the parents' difficulties, a deeper root. Another scene may lurk in the background.

Marie's temper tantrum makes such an impression on Evelyn because it reminds her of another violent scene, with other actors, long ago in her own past. The particular strangeness that upsets Mrs. Martin is due to the furtive appearance of ghosts from her own past. These ghosts create the same anxious suspense we feel at the movies when, behind the hero, a mysterious shadow looms up that only we viewers can see. In the therapy session, the movie hero is the mother of the baby, the fascinated spectator is the therapist, and the disturbing shadow is the ghost of the mother's mother (or another member of her immediate family).

We can see this shadow as the first meeting with Mrs. Martin continues.

"What's more," she says, "there's a kind of aggressiveness that I just can't cope with. When I tell her not to do something, she honestly gets quite vicious. She scratches me or bites me, or else she hits me. When that happens, I just don't know what to do. I don't think that slapping her is the answer."

In an attempt to get closer to the reason why she is so upset, I tell Mrs. Martin that it must be a surprise to her when a tiny little thing like Marie is so rough. "That must have been pretty unexpected," I say to her, encouraging her to talk about the gap between her expectations for her imaginary baby and the surprise the real one caused.

"Yes, I didn't expect this. It's like a battle of wills. It's as if she was trying to see how far she can push me."

Inwardly, I am astonished that a grown woman should feel she was being challenged by this tiny, motionless infant who looks more like a little bird than an ogre. The discrepancy between the intimidation felt by the mother and the peaceful little girl that I see before me gives me a hint that another scene, perhaps a nightmare, blurs the image Mrs. Martin has of her daughter.

Mrs. Martin says she is very worried that she and

Marie might reach a "point of no return." She is afraid that if she gave her child a spanking, Marie might one day say, "My mother is a torturer, she's not a mother."

I am struck by the exaggeration of this torturer image, which confirms that a fantasy of great violence is terrorizing this mother. And at this point the whole stage shifts; the key moves from major to minor, the backdrop changes, and an enormous, ill-defined but frightening character bursts onto the stage.

It is twenty years earlier: Mrs. Martin's past is catapulted into the interview room and we are all about to watch in amazement the violent dissent that pitted Evelyn Martin against her own mother from the outset of *their* relationship.

Mrs. Martin has lost her smile. She becomes increasingly disturbed as she explains: "I had . . . well my mother was pretty impatient. It didn't take much for her to grab the carpet-beater . . . so I have to say I have some pretty bad memories of her. I even used to hide things from her because I was afraid how she'd take them. I don't want Marie to get that way. There was a time, when I was still living at home, when things got pretty violent."

And then with great emotion in her voice she says, "No, I really . . . I really don't want to have that kind of relationship with Marie." Her tone is one of deep anxiety, as if she were convinced that nothing could stop the two of them from fulfilling their destiny of shared violence.

Now, only eight minutes into our session, already the present reality of Marie and her problems has been left behind. A ghost has taken the infant's place: an old event has taken the place of the temper tantrum in the restaurant.

The Child as Double

A new character has settled in among us, looming larger with each act in the drama, growing stronger in color, clearer in outline. This character climbs back to life out of the confining catacombs of Evelyn Martin's childhood memories.

The disquieting strangeness Evelyn had felt is the result of the unrecognized presence of this ghost hidden behind the child. The violence Evelyn sees in Marie is probably the violence she experienced with her own mother. And as we will see, Evelyn's complaints about Marie were in fact directed at the baby's grandmother. Evelyn Martin complains about her mother's violence *through* Marie, who is merely a substitute, a stand-in for her grandmother. Marie is her grandmother's "double," and she terrorizes Evelyn Martin just as the woman she replaces did.

The Fear of Madness

Evelyn Martin, however, does not yet acknowledge this ghost, and she goes on to suggest a perfectly reasonable and (to her) more acceptable basis for this terror: Marie may not be normal. After she has described her fear of the violent behavior that typified her relations with her mother, Evelyn pulls herself together, stops for a minute (as if to ward off the ghost that has just put in an appearance), switches off the lights that had illuminated the scene with the carpet-beater, then asks me, "So, in the tests they did on Marie, did they find anything abnormal?" Slightly taken aback, I remember that she is consulting me as a specialist, and I reassure her that all the test results are normal. But I go on to make a connection: I suggest that Evelyn is asking me this question about the tests because she's afraid there is something abnormal about Marie. And, furthermore, what she fears deep down is that she has already in fact reproduced with Marie the violent relationship she had had with her own mother.

Evelyn Martin agrees but then introduces a new character: her husband is very concerned about Marie's violent behavior. Some remarks made by friends had increased the parents' fear that Marie might be a bit mentally abnormal.

I am very pleased that this worry has been put into words. Fear of madness is everywhere: we all have it, for ourselves and for others. It is crucial that the fear be recognized, then clarified, so that it can be exorcised.

In fact, more or less consciously, all parents have worried about having an "abnormal" child. It happens particularly during the last trimester of pregnancy, but this specter can raise its head at any stage in development—when the baby cries too loudly, when a child refuses to go to school, when there are problems at school, or when a teenager's behavior becomes too outrageous.

Many people fear psychiatrists, and stubbornly *avoid* consulting one, because they have the deep, unspoken conviction that psychiatry will confirm their fears that their child is mad.

Well, in the present case, it was easy for me to do the opposite and to exorcise the anxiety: the fear of madness in fact covered over the fear of reproducing today the violence of yesterday. In our childhoods, we have all known feelings of violence, of extremes of passion and hatred. When such feelings reemerge, they are always experienced as a threat to psychic equilibrium, as harbingers of madness.

Often this hidden content need only be given a name and the fear of madness will vanish. This is precisely what happened when Evelyn Martin discovered that her real fear was to involve Marie in such a violent relationship that they would reach a point of no return and reproduce Evelyn's own past with her mother.

By identifying this ancient drama, by pointing out the way it is being repeated in the present, we can exorcise the frightening ghost and reduce the fear of madness.

Simply by showing Mrs. Martin that she was afraid of becoming, in her turn, her daughter's "torturer," a first level of anguish could be relieved. In this way I could reassure her that she was not inexorably bound to repeat the past, that her fate was not necessarily to become in her turn the mother-torturer that she had so much feared.

A new freedom was hers for the taking: she would look upon Marie with different eyes.

The "Encounter Effect"

Everything that I have described so far was wholly contained in the first ten minutes of our first interview. In those few minutes, a woman confided to a stranger an essential part of the drama of her past life, and her chief cause of concern for her baby.

She had never told this to anyone else, and she had no idea that on this particular day she was going to reveal so much.

There is in the encounter with a nonjudgmental professional therapist, ready to listen and vested with the power of science, an astonishingly revelatory effect: this is the "encounter effect."

A pediatric visit often lasts no longer than ten minutes. Many such appointments are made out of concerns and problems similar to those I have just sketched out. However, in ten minutes the pediatrician cannot get involved in the discovery process that was set in motion in the Martins' case. The pediatrician must deal with the most pressing issue, that is, the baby's "symptom." Since, as in Marie's case, the "symptom" seems innocuous, the doctor will tend automatically in most cases to reassure the parent, give some advice or a prescription, and top the whole thing off with the ritual phrase, "Just wait, it's only a phase."

In many cases, the pediatrician's reassuring attitude will be enough to calm the underlying anxiety. But obviously in a case like Marie's, reassurance and, above all, a prescription cannot solve the problem of Marie's "aggressiveness."

Fortunately, on this occasion, the pediatrician understood that psychic, not physical, pain was the problem. Lacking the reservations that classical medicine often has with regard to psychiatry, he preferred to refer for a psychiatric consultation, sensing—thanks to his experience and sensitivity—that Mrs. Martin was ready to attempt some self-reflection. In some cases, pediatricians trained in "behavioral pediatrics" or psychiatry will take the time to explore such issues, in their milder form, themselves.

Mrs. Martin was thus already prepared to accept that the problem was not purely physical or requiring special parenting methods. As we have seen, her state of mind could be characterized as worried questioning. She did not understand her child and was ready to address the issue of *her* relation to the baby. This was evident when she took only ten minutes to express a deep-rooted concern, bound up with another mother-child relationship, the one she had known herself.

This discovery of the past relationship in the present became possible for her because I did not offer reassurance or advice when I listened to her complaints and thus allowed the "encounter effect" to operate.

But now we will see why one cannot stop at this first gleam of enlightenment even if it has led to an easing of anxiety. A ten-minute interview can change a lot of things, but in a psychotherapeutic investigation we have to go further.

Layer upon Layer

In psychoanalysis we learn that any psychic manifestation—be it a feeling, a fantasy, or an anxiety—is multileveled. Something on one level may conceal its opposite: a fear may reveal a wish, just as a wish may mask an evasion.

The way someone expresses a concern may yield a first meaning (our red thread) that—when the patient is free to follow her stream of consciousness—will bring out other, more hidden, meanings. Like an onion, the psyche can be peeled back to reveal a series of meanings, one on top of another, with the most unconscious meanings deep in the core.

Thus in psychoanalysis one never gets to *the* fundamental cause. The therapist's art consists in endlessly seeking what is not expressed in the succession of utterances the patient produces.

So far with Mrs. Martin and Marie, we had successfully defined a first theme: the fear of finding, with Marie, the violence that characterized Evelyn's relationship with her own mother during her childhood. We shall see that Evelyn's perception that "Marie is attacking me" hides other concerns that will emerge progressively. One fear may hide another, one visible sign hides a deeper one, and the therapist's work consists in making possible a series of multiple reversals.

Violence and Love

One of the commonest, and most disturbing, reversals is the change from hate to love. At the first stage, I might have been content to explain Mrs. Martin's initial complaints about Marie in terms of the fear of violence between a mother and her daughter. On the face of it, it would be quite natural for Mrs. Martin to reproduce with Marie the violence, even the hatred, that lay at the heart of her relation with her mother, together with the host of anxieties left by that experience.

Soon, however, this theory had to be abandoned. Following the first ten minutes that had filled our stage with quarrels between mothers and daughters, a new song was to be heard.

Guilt

We had just finished talking about the arguments between Evelyn and her mother. Marie starts moving: she puts her hand up to her mother's face and touches her glasses. Mrs. Martin jerks backward, takes off her glasses, and says firmly to Marie, "No, no!" I sense that she is afraid of the baby's sudden movement, and I tell her that she is interpreting this gesture as provoking an aggressive confrontation. I add that she is constantly afraid that the same fights will be repeated with Marie that she had experienced with her mother and which she still remembers so bitterly.

Mrs. Martin agrees: "Sometimes things really got out of hand between us. Once I even slapped my mother back. I really wouldn't like my daughter to slap me. My mother had the mark of my five fingers on her face."

That slap has indeed left a deep mark: Mrs. Martin's mother wept when it happened. Shortly afterwards Evelyn Martin was sent to a boarding school, where she was to remain for four years (from the age of thirteen to seventeen).

This feeling of guilt is intensely painful. How could she, as a thirteen-year-old girl, slap her own mother? And the punishment was not slow in coming: exile to a boarding school, then a progressive and irreversible distance between Evelyn and her mother.

What a reversal! At stage one we could assume simply that Mrs. Martin was terrorized by the "violence" in Marie, as she had been by her mother's carpet-beater. She had been the victim, the others were the torturers. It is a simple formula, one we often hear today: a life is marked indelibly by the experience of violence. Yet now Mrs. Martin turns out herself to have been guilty of an act of abuse as indelible as the mark of five fingers blazing on her mother's face as she left to go to work.

The initial picture has already changed a lot. And yet, we are only in the sixteenth minute of this first interview. In a few minutes, a scene dating back some ten years has obscured the present, just as a flow of lava destroys a familiar landscape during a volcanic eruption.

The roles Evelyn and her daughter have been given are no longer so simple: If she fears Marie's aggressiveness, isn't it because her daughter is stirring up memories of her own violence against her mother, and thus causing unbearable guilt? Perhaps her fears are the result of the following unconscious prophecy: Marie also will slap her mother, leading to a rupture and exile to a boarding school.

Evelyn Martin will confirm this: it is since her daughter has been having her "fits of violence" that she herself has thought back to the time she slapped her mother in the kitchen, and to the marks of her fingers that she cannot manage to erase from her memory. "If she goes on like this, she too might go that far." A scene of violence that had long been dormant looms up as a result of Marie's presence. That would indeed be the worst of punishments for Evelyn, that the slap that made her lose contact with her mother may one day cause her to break with Marie. Such a prospect is indeed frightening.

An eye for an eye. . . . She has sinned by striking her mother. She will be punished by being struck in her turn. This is the logic of wrongdoing. In this way, the theme of guilt creeps like a shadow from behind the initial complaints about Marie's violence. This is a first reversal, and to come to terms with it we must move on to another, even more unexpected, theme.

Nostalgia for Love

Nostalgia is one of the most powerful human passions.
Nothing is sweeter than the evocation of the lost paradise of childhood. Nothing is more seductive than
imagining the loves one has inspired (or thinks one
has inspired).

Nostalgia is almost always associated with the
image of an idyllic relationship, both exclusive and una-
dulterated, with the perfect parent, usually the mother.

We can find this image in all cultures, all eras, in
art, in religion, in philosophy. Museums are full of moving images of all-powerful mothers and maternal love.
Many religions represent the supreme goddess in the
shape of the fertile mother. Even though Judeo-
Christian tradition shows a decided preference for the
father-son relationship, the cult of Mary, mother of
Jesus, represents a chance of intercession, of warmth
and comfort, balancing the severity of a demanding
heavenly father. The Catholic church realized at an early
stage how necessary it is for us to have recourse to a
maternal image and therefore chose to call itself the
"mother church." Christian Science uses the same term.

This nostalgia for the past forms an essential motivation for people's decision to become parents. The desire to re-create an ideal parent-child relationship such as

one has experienced or would like to have experienced inspires men and women barely out of puberty with the ambition to become parents. A very ancient relationship, swallowed up in an individual's prehistory, will undergo a transformation and drive a man or a woman to re-create a parent-child relationship. This individual may never realize that it is the child lost in the mists of personal prehistory who presides over his or her fate as a parent. But if a problem arises, a process of self-discovery (such as may occur in psychotherapy) reveals the connection between the relationship currently being established with the baby and the relationship that presided over the dawn of the parent's own infancy.

Fueled by nostalgia, prehistory is reproduced in the present; the past repeats itself today; the child is father to the man, and every mother rediscovers aspects of her first relationship when she becomes a mother.

This is why so many mothers dream about their own mothers soon after they have given birth. Others see things in their babies that remind them of their mothers. One mother I was following in analysis used to tell me that she could hear her mother's voice when her baby whimpered. When this kind of thing happens, it means that early relationships in the mother's childhood are being revived in order to facilitate the new mother-baby relationship.

It doesn't matter that now it is a baby who represents the mother's mother. What counts is that the primary love relationship is being revived, that the experience of love today takes the place of a nostalgia for love yesterday.

The plan to have a child contains a promise of recapturing an experience that has been buried for too long. Becoming a parent is thus a way to rediscover *one's own* parents.

Exile

We have all been cast out from the lost paradise of primary love. But for some of us exile takes place brutally following a quarrel, as a result of distance, or because of death.

For Evelyn Martin, exile was a heavy, real-life sorrow. Despairing of ever achieving a satisfying rapport with her parents, she had decided to leave home at the age of twenty-two. "One day," she says, "I packed my bags and walked out on my mother, the poor thing." Evelyn felt bad about "walking out" on her mother, but living like a stranger in the same house had become too frustrating.

Since that time, she had seen little of her parents and they in fact had moved some six hundred miles away to their native Spain. At this point in the story a new surprise emerges and another radical reversal occurs. Whereas one might rightly have expected

Evelyn to blossom in the newfound peace and freedom her parents' absence afforded her, in fact she starts to lament about her parents being so far away. She was the one who had packed her bags, but now she was suffering from her exile. Once again I was reminded that the nostalgia for love can never be assuaged: despite all the conflicts that had painfully divided her from her mother, Evelyn still dreamed every day that her mother would reach out to her, make contact.

This is how we came to the following event that occurred at the end of the first interview. Evelyn had begun complaining again about the way Marie was so rough with her. At this point a short scene took place, illustrating how bitterly dissatisfied Evelyn felt. Marie puts her hand to her mother's mouth and Evelyn draws back, saying, "You almost scratched me then." Since I could not see any hostility in the child's gesture, I comment to Evelyn, "You seem to be expecting her to take revenge on you at any minute." Evelyn responds: "Yes, it's automatic. She almost never shows any affection for me. Sometimes, when you give someone a hug, it would be nice if they hugged you back!"

Here at last is the root of Evelyn's complaints: she expects Marie to show her some affection, and she complains in an almost childish way. It's as if she were hurt because her baby doesn't return her caresses. Clearly it is the child in Evelyn who is complaining, and the target of the complaint, we now realize, cannot be

Marie. We are dealing here with her first love: her mother.

At that point Evelyn embarks on a new series of woes. She tells me that she sees her mother very rarely, only during vacations, and even then her mother has to be shared with the rest of the family.

I suggest at this point that the reason why Evelyn is so fearful of a split between herself and Marie is that she feels deep nostalgia for her mother. She responds immediately: "That is so true. If she called me today, saying she was coming, I would be over the moon." She adds that the bond she has to her parents can never be broken, that she is always hoping a reunion will be possible, that she feels like an outcast doomed to be forever homesick.

Evelyn goes on to assert—to my surprise—that her mother also is very attached to her: "When I am with them there, she starts to cry three days before I leave!"

How many opportunities for love have been lost, how many encounters missed between this daughter and her mother? Apparently, the only way these two women can communicate is by arguing, and resentment is the currency of their love.

Reversals

What a series of reversals has occurred in the course of this first conversation! It begins with the mother complaining that her thirteen-month-old daughter is excessively rough. It ends with her confessing that for twenty years she has harbored love for her own mother who lives six hundred miles away.

Such rapid switches (from violence to love, from baby to grandmother) feature in all these conversations with parents and child. We can state a general rule: the parents' complaints about their baby (or later about their child or their teenager) are, at bottom, addressed to each parent's own parents. When a baby is born, the frustrations, the rancor, the resentments arising out of the parent's childhood relationships with his or her own parents are carried over onto the baby. One might even say that this transference of ancient relationships onto the baby is analogous to the transference that forces the patient to treat his analyst like a new edition of his parents. The baby becomes the effigy of his grandparents. The relationship with the baby offers a new venue for the drama played out in the parent's childhood. This is how psychological inheritances are passed on in families.

We shall discuss this later on, when we look in detail at family traits and what is called "psychological heredity."

Scenarios for Mother and Baby

By the end of my first conversation with Evelyn Martin, I felt I had been watching a minidrama that involved several characters (some of whom were not in the consulting room) and several themes, each of which had a logical thread of its own. The way the mother and the baby interacted had a programmed quality. The theme of "Marie is rough and shows her mother no affection" keeps reappearing in some action where the baby "scratches" her mother's face.

This theme is repeated so often that it seems to shape this whole mother-child relationship, leading the mother to seek professional help. A theatrical metaphor remains useful as we consider the repetitive, compulsive nature of this theme. There are roles (victim, villain), a well-organized sequence of events, and, above all, a script that turns out to have been written a long time ago (in the mother's childhood). We seem to be watching a performance of a play by actors who faithfully recite a preestablished text. There is little room for improvisation: everything seems set up in advance.

The preexistence of the script, the rehearsal of the key-sequence, the impression that the main characters are strictly limited by their assigned parts, and, last, the way this minidrama is acted out by two people before our eyes, all this bears out the analogy with a play's script.

Interactions of this kind indicate that *every relationship* between parent and child is influenced by such scenarios, more or less compulsively, more or less problematically.

The scenario has a content—in the shape of ideas, fantasies, feelings—and a form that is acted out (the interactions). The content varies, according to the ups and downs of the parent's relationship with his or her own parents. It is also molded, as we will see, by the baby's own individual character. Some babies, for example, are supersensitive: they keep crying no matter what is done to calm them down, they reject their food, they shudder every time they are touched.

Babies like this will be especially frustrating for a mother who already feels that she has been unable to satisfy her parents.

Many mothers worry that their babies will suffer from some problem or defect, some more than others. If that problem should then arise in actual fact—if, for example, the baby turns out to have some illness or birth defect—a dramatic, and perhaps irreversible, breakdown occurs in certain mother-baby pairs.

The effects of such poorly fitting combinations can be devastating. I have seen mothers filled with despair, convinced that they are incompetent, useless even. This kind of vicious cycle tends to go on autopilot. The terrified mothers are sure they have proof that they and their children are doomed to failure and unhappiness. In such cases, my task will be to uncover the dominant scenario, i.e., the theme rooted in the mother's unconscious history and acted out by two actors who feel more anxiety than pleasure in their roles. Then we have to get down to causes and break the chains of fatality. Later in this book we shall see how it is possible to conjure away what may feel like an evil spell and even radically alter the scenarios written by the previous generation.

Fortunately, most scenarios are not determined by the need to fail and do not lead to a life of unhappiness. Contrary to general belief, happiness too has a history. Some babies are lucky enough to make the dearest dreams of their parents come true. They may, for example, be born at the exact time when their parents needed to find a certain type of baby—the type they happen to be. By reason of appearance, sex, or temperament, an infant can come along to make real an ideal of perfection that parents have been seeking. Then everything is simple. Each stage in development confirms the parental expectations: the script unfolds according to plan and reality confirms the fantasy. A feeling of reciprocity arises whereby parents and child are justified in their certainty that they have found their ideal partner. This reciprocity is the basis for a fundamental confidence that nothing can shake. Men and women have often risen to greatness, inspired by the conviction that theirs will be an exceptional destiny, because of that magical combination of complete mutual satisfaction they enjoyed with their parents.

A Chance to Change the Script

Biography as well as psychiatric practice teaches us that
these scenarios—which can be called transgenera-
tional—exert a considerable and lasting influence. They
shape the first relationships but also persist throughout
life.

Each one of us is trying to work with these influences. Our life plans, our choices, as well as our failures
and our depressions, are inscribed in the logic of these
scripts. Thus it is important for each of us to decipher
the code, to track down its source, and, insofar as this
is possible, to control the way it affects our real-life
actions.

Very early childhood is the ideal time to uncover
the first outlines of these scenarios. In fact, the plans
that parents have for their child are particularly visible in
the postpartum period. When these plans have gone
awry, consultations with parents and baby offer an
extraordinary opportunity to influence a destiny while
it is still malleable. The bets are still being laid, the
patterns have not yet become fixed and automatic. Thus
these early relationships offer a choice arena in which
psychiatrists and students of child development can
work on prevention rather than cure.

As an infant psychiatrist I feel fortunate to be able
to have some influence very early on, before the dia-

logue between parent and child breaks down, before failure and lack of communication are locked in.

Learning the Script

One fundamental question has always fascinated me. If these scenarios have such a profound influence on a relationship, and if it is true that the baby plays exactly the part he or she has been cast in, how is the infant taught the script? How does it come about that the baby acts precisely in the expected way?

It is often possible to watch babies faithfully perform the script laid out in advance in their mothers' personal history. How do they get to know the parts they must play? How does it happen that a mother who fears coldness has a baby who is aloof with her? How do we explain the fact that a mother whose chief anxiety centers on feeding has an anorexic baby? Or that the baby of a mother who, above all, fears to be abandoned learns to be afraid every time he is separated from her?

Let us look at one striking example. A young mother seeks advice because her baby keeps throwing up. Her worries seem quite out of proportion because the baby is thriving. When you listen to what this mother says, it turns out that she sees a connection between her baby's eating and the death of her brother, which occurred in the last trimester of her pregnancy. "What did your brother die of?" "Stomach cancer," the mother replies, and she describes her brother's struggle at the end, and how awful it was to see him vomit. At this very point in the interview, the baby throws up! The coincidence makes it easy to make the connection. "The reason you're so worried about your baby vomiting is because you interpret this as the first sign of a fatal illness." The effect is instantaneous. As soon as the worrying incident has been deciphered in terms of some former situation that has not been worked through, the anxiety abates. The mother had confused her son and her brother. Once the connection has been made, she is able to weep—for the first time since her brother died—and her worries about the baby disappear.

However, the question to ask next must be the following: Is the baby's throwing up—at the same time that his mother is describing her brother's vomiting—somehow engineered by his mother as evidence to prove her confusions between son/brother and vomiting/cancer? Do we assume that the mother "asks" the child to act out a symptom or behavior that would underline his resemblance to the brother, thus allowing the mother to find once again the dead brother she had been incapable of mourning? By this hypothesis, the baby would play a part in which he reincarnates a person the mother needs to find. The astonishing thing is that a baby is able to perceive the maternal request and comply with it. How can a baby know the part that his mother wants him to play?

Other similar cases have convinced me that parents can handle their children physically in such a way that they induce regurgitations (though it is still necessary for the baby to be predisposed to regurgitate, a not uncommon thing). The way of holding a baby (head down, for example), of bouncing him around (for example with overexciting games), or else some kind of excessively intense stimulation can all serve to induce regurgitation. The way the baby is fed must also be taken into account, as this can cause him to gag and spit up.

There are some mothers, for example, who are so afraid that their babies will die of hunger that they stuff food into them, ignoring all the signals the baby may give. In doing this, the mothers disturb the babies' hunger rhythm, thereby again inducing regurgitations.

In the earlier story, the child's throwing up at the very moment when his mother is describing her dying brother seemed to me a form of communication: the baby produces his symptom just when his mother is describing the same symptom in her brother. The baby is sensitive to his mother's distress and molds his behavior to fit the part she asks him to play.

A number of symptoms and behavior patterns appear to be a baby's response to an unconscious expectation on the parents' part and to their emotional state. Babies speak with their bodies. If this is true, we need to entertain the idea that babies are sensitive to their mothers' state of mind and that some mutual communication is set up between them. Evidence that this is indeed the case will be explored in the next chapter.

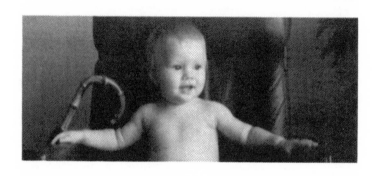

THREE

Babies as Gifted Actors

❦

How Does the Message Get Through?

As we have seen, babies somehow tune in to the messages transmitted to them by their mothers and seem to accept the roles in which their mothers have cast them. While babies don't understand words the way an adult would, neither do they tune in to their mothers by magic. So, how is meaning conveyed between mother and infant?

Instead of words, mother and baby have another kind of vocabulary. Each little part of the daily routine that knits mother and baby together carries the message of the scenarios that they act out.

If babies are to tune in to these "messages," certain conditions have to be fulfilled. First, the baby has to have bonded with his or her mother and chosen her as the partner upon whom to rely totally. Second, babies have to have some intelligence, have to under-stand that all the things they perceive about their mothers—voice, face, gestures—make up a whole and belong to one and the same person.

As adults we are obviously able to determine that such and such a voice, or expression, or movement are attributes of one single, familiar person. However, is it equally obvious that a baby only a few weeks old can link one isolated event (the sound of a voice, for exam-ple) to a whole (a person)? In other words, can babies recognize their mothers? Such recognition is an essential precondition if we are to prove that a baby reacts to all the signals given out by the mother on whom he or she depends so closely. As we shall see, babies are indeed able to perceive their mothers as whole persons.

The next essential precondition is that babies be able to see some pattern in their exchanges with moth-ers, enabling them to become familiar with and learn to predict them. Predictability is crucial if a baby is to adapt to a familiar "code of behavior" that sets up the conventions shaping interactions. Adults are equally sen-sitive to the conventions regulating social intercourse: any unexpected deviation from the norm (such as a kiss from a stranger) is a shock. We shall see that very young babies have already gained this ability to predict patterns in social behavior and are surprised if any rules are violated.

Last, we shall see that the baby is sensitive to the

mother's emotional messages, that he knows when she is worried or glad, when she approves or disapproves of what he is doing.

Babies as People

Only in the last few decades have babies been credited with any authentic mental functions. Hitherto they were seen as passive creatures, to be fed and cared for and taught how to do things. Continuing research has established a new image for the baby as someone capable of intention, discrimination, attachment, and evasion, gifted with complex perceptual abilities, and sensitive to the way exchanges with a mother are set up. Since it was discovered that very young infants are hypersensitive to interactions with their partners, we can no longer look on a baby as a household plant that simply needs light and nourishment. The baby has become a person.

Research has shown conclusively that very early on, newborn infants can recognize their mothers. T. Berry Brazelton—who pioneered this research—likes to give a demonstration of this fact to young mothers. On the third day after the birth, as part of a test called the Brazelton Neonatal Behavioral Assessment Scale, he shows that the infant turns his head 180 degrees to track a colored object or follow the sound of a bell. Then he picks up the baby, with one hand under the child's head and the other under his bottom, and holds him out toward his mother, telling her to call out the baby's name, while he does the same thing. Invariably, after two or three attempts, the baby turns his face toward the mother! It's as if he has already recognized his mother. Every time I have seen this demonstration, the mother has been deeply moved, sometimes bursting into tears as she realizes that her voice has power and that her child has chosen her.

In the first days after birth, a baby will take a longer sniff of a breastpad soaked in his mother's milk than of one soaked in cow's milk. From the age of two months, infants will stare longer at a drawing of a human face than at one in which all the elements in the drawing—nose, mouth, eyes, and so on—are mixed up.

Infants therefore are not only able to recognize the human face, but they can distinguish certain attributes associated with their mothers. These abilities will help them to become preferentially attached to their mothers, who shower them with attention and thereby set up patterns of exchange.

Constructing the Mother's Image

However, does the baby know that the voice and the face of the mother are parts of a single entity? And how will the infant make the connection between some service the mother performs for him (such as feeding) and attachment to the person of the mother? Such questions are important, for if syntheses of this kind failed to occur, the baby would be living in a fragmented world, made up of isolated acts and experiences. (Fragmentation of this kind accounts in part for the strange world inhabited by autistic children.)

No simple answer is possible to the question of how infants integrate their mothers into a single entity, as so many factors come into play in complex mental representations. What can be demonstrated is that babies can put together a sound and a picture. For example, in one experiment, a four-month-old baby is shown two films simultaneously, about three inches apart. One film features a facial close-up of someone playing "Peekaboo." The other film shows a hand beating a drum.

When the two films are projected with a single soundtrack (the voice saying "Peekaboo" or the drumbeat), the baby looks selectively at the film where sound and picture are in agreement. When he hears the drumbeat, the baby looks toward the drum; when he hears the voice, he turns toward the picture of the face. The baby manages to establish what sound corresponds to what picture and realizes the equivalence between two stimuli provided by two different senses. This is called cross-modal equivalence.

All of this research may seem to be proving the

obvious, but in fact we have here an extraordinary phenomenon that is very difficult to explain. How does the baby know right from the start that there is an equivalence between a sound and a picture or, more exactly, between a sound sequence and a visual sequence?

We have no answer to that question, but we do know the extraordinary potential that this capacity for concordance and synthesis represents in the development of intelligence and mental functioning. It is this type of capacity that will permit substitutions to occur: when infants hear their mothers' voices, they "know" that this sound is one part of the reality called mother. A part will represent the whole.

This synthesizing ability will play a part in the construction of more and more complete images of the mother and of the infant's environment. Babies will know that the voice, face, and embrace of their mothers are not separate units or disparate experiences. They will have the potential to construct an integrated image of their mothers, built from a thousand different clues.

Furthermore, this synthetic ability facilitates communication by permitting a kind of translation, on the baby's part, of certain things the mother does. William Condon and Louis Sander were the first to show that babies can synchronize their motions to the mother's voice. Let's imagine a baby who is very excited by a game she is playing with her mother and that she expresses this by vigorously waving her arms and legs.

The mother, delighted to see the pleasure she is giving her child, reacts in her turn but in a different modality. Instead of using her body, she will say "Ah, *that's* my baby!" raising her voice and stressing the word *that's*. Daniel Stern (1985) has called this "affect attunement."

For an external observer, there is no doubt about what is happening: the rising curve of the mother's vocalization is a spoken response to the baby's rising limbs. It is as if she were, in her own way, reproducing the baby's excited movements. It's the beginning of "conversation."

The baby is able to "understand" the equivalence between her mother's exclamation and her own movements only if she is capable of transferring information from one modality to another. She makes the connection between what she heard (her mother's voice) and what she did (waved her arms around) in just the same way as she linked the sound of the drum with the picture of the drum in the experiment discussed earlier.

Why is this ability to "translate" so important to infants?

It is important because it makes it possible for them to know that their mothers have understood them, even if mothers express themselves in quite a different modality. When the baby hears her mother say "Ah, *that's* my baby!" in a voice that rises just as her own excitement had risen, she receives evidence that her mother shared her experience, that someone has responded as she does. In other words, she moves out of solitude and knows she is in communion with another being. This is the first stage in communication, the start of a dialogue that, later on, will progress into spoken language, the most evolved means we have to share our experiences. (There are other means to share experience—acts of love, dancing, the emotion shared before a work of art—but speech when it is fully developed allows far greater areas of experience to be covered.)

The realm of communication between infant and mother is full of mystery. How do newborn babies make their mothers understand their needs and desires? Correspondingly, how does a mother manage to get her needs through to the baby?

In other words, why is it that mothers and babies do not move along, side by side, each absorbed in his or her own individual references, needs, and challenges? After all, the world of an adult and the world of an infant are so very different. How does it come about that some kind of harmony—however relative—grows up between mother and baby most of the time? Some specialists have claimed that the infant is autistic, that is, a being wholly closed in upon himself, incapable of attending to a partner, wholly immersed in the determinism of his inner world. (Certain children never manage to establish communication with their human partners: they remain without language or without dialogue. These children are truly autistic.) Now, whereas it is

certainly true that a newborn baby sleeps about twenty
hours a day and seems to react largely to internal stimuli, nonetheless, from the first days of life, windows of
attentiveness open up, times when the baby is receptive
to social—yes, social—exchange and takes note of other
people and what they are doing. What is it that makes
these moments of dialogue possible? What is it that
makes the baby a human being, a social animal?

And, more fundamentally, what is it that allows
babies progressively to perceive that they themselves are
the source of these needs and wishes? How will they be
able to convey the nature and intensity of these needs
to another being who can be counted on to recognize,
accept, and satisfy them?

How does it come about that—gradually—babies
see themselves as *persons*? Eventually a baby will be able
to use the word *I* to refer to himself or herself and *you*
for the person he or she will negotiate with to get
needs met (something the truly autistic child does not
manage). Language develops only if infants realize not
only that they have needs but also that they have been
conveyed effectively to someone else.

Pas de Deux

When the ways babies and mothers behave together are
analyzed in great detail, it becomes possible to represent

graphically that there is a constant interchange between what the baby does and what the mother does. Such studies are called "microanalyses," since they set out to record extremely short interactions, a few tenths of a second long.

Together with Edward Tronick, Brazelton has shown that in normal circumstances mother and baby adapt to each other, as they follow a rhythmic pattern of mutual engagement and withdrawal. They become mutually stimulated in a game, following a rising curve, then calm down, and at last establish a distance between them. When these cycles are graphed, one obtains rising and falling curves, in the form of waves. Here is visual evidence that a rhythm has been set up and that—for each mother-baby couple—a characteristic and repetitive shape of interaction is sketched out. It is as if the two were engaged in a dance where each partner anticipates the movements of the other, bowing to the shared rhythm, and relying on the predictability of the music.

When this systematic, predictable aspect of the "interactive dance" was first demonstrated, it made a great impact on researchers in the field. Previously it had been assumed that the baby was sensitive only to the pressure of inner needs such as hunger, fatigue, or discomfort. No one had realized that the baby was sensitive to social exchanges. Condon, Sander, Brazelton, and others succeeded in demonstrating that an interactive structure is put in place very early in life. As is the case with adults, interactions for babies are not haphazard but arise out of a system created by mother and child in partnership. Moreover, each partner has a body language. Mother and baby seem able to interpret movements in terms of intention: this gesture means "she wants to play," that one "we have to stop." Physical interaction becomes communication.

Gradually baby and mother set up some kind of guidelines determining what each can expect from the other, what is okay, what is a "no-no." This reciprocal adaptation has been labeled "synchrony."

As we shall see, the messages can be far more complex yet. The baby will be capable of reading into his mother's behavior such meanings as: "I have to be lively to entertain her," "I have to avoid touching her," "She does not like me to move away," "She won't allow me to get really excited." Thus, interactions have become communication codes that mother and baby decipher and that determine their actions.

Furthermore, the predictability of these interactive sequences is so strong that the baby reacts as soon as there is a change. Any variations the mother introduces will enlarge the vocabulary of that communication. But if the variation is too abrupt, it amounts to a violation of the convention and the baby reacts with distress. This has been demonstrated with the experiments done by Brazelton, Tronick, and colleagues, known as "still face." After the mother has been asked to sit facing her baby and to play normally, she is given the signal to stop all her movements, vocalizations, and imitations. She becomes "still-faced." A baby's first reaction is surprise, then he or she tries to get some reaction from the mother; after twenty seconds, the baby becomes upset, then falls into a kind of apathy. This experiment has shown how very sensitive the baby is to the predictability of exchanges, and that any violation of the usual convention results in astonishment and distress. Further experiments like this have confirmed these discoveries. Interactions between mother and baby have a structure and are used by both to convey their feelings and intentions.

The existence of this systematization of interactions explains why the baby is so sensitive to the changes affecting the mother. Any variation in the interaction becomes a message, and the gestures, vocalizations, and positions of the mother are all signs in this system of protocommunication. The scenarios we have been describing are "written" in this expressive early language.

The Contract

We have now seen that, from an early age, babies are tuned in not only to the messages their mothers are sending but also to the structure of the interactions. It seems that babies soon learn how to adapt to the boundaries of the exchange, how to alternate roles, how to fall in with a special rhythm of interactive sequences. Studies on language acquisition have suggested that the baby is sensitive even to the rules that determine the exchange. Some form of convention is established between each mother and child, regulating what is allowed, what is forbidden, what is mandatory. One could say that a kind of contract is negotiated. Babies learn what terms they must respect to maintain their relationship with their mothers. This contract is binding, since a baby needs to be reassured at every moment by the mother's expression or tone of voice that she is pleased with him or her. It's as if the baby were equipped with radar, constantly trying to scan the mother's face for evidence that he or she pleases and satisfies her completely. The search for that approval is so intense that the baby is always alert for every sign, always in suspense.

Reading the Mother's Face

Experiments have proved that babies can successfully decode certain facial characteristics, in particular the affective value of certain expressions. For example, at five months, babies can match up a happy expression and a happy tone of voice, a sad expression and a sad tone of voice. They "know" that the sad expression belongs to the same set as the sad voice.

In the course of the second part of the first year, babies become particularly attentive to the mother's facial expressions: their behavior will in fact be shaped by these expressions. The following experiment makes this quite clear. A baby is set down on a surface covered by a thick sheet of glass. At the opposite end of the glass is a very attractive toy. Without fail, the baby begins to crawl toward the toy, but when he has gotten halfway, he is faced with a dilemma. The ground *beneath* the glass drops off suddenly, and the baby has the impression that he is on the edge of a cliff. In fact, of course, there is no danger since he is still on the glass slab, and nothing prevents him from reaching the toy. Still, the baby notices the change beneath him, he thinks he is facing an unfamiliar obstacle, and his reaction is typical. He looks surprised, as if he has been faced with something he can't figure out, but he is still attracted by the toy. Each time, the baby looks back at his mother, who is behind him, and inspects her face. This inspection is so automatic that it seems almost like a reflex. If he is unsure or nervous, the baby's radar turns on automatically and it is quite clear that he expects to learn from his mother's face *what he should be feeling and doing.*

At this critical moment, there are two possibilities. The mother can smile and encourage the baby to keep going after the toy: she does this wholly by facial expressions since she has been forbidden to use words or gestures. When this happens, the baby seems reassured and starts off again, merrily walking over the apparent cliff to get to the toy he wants. If, however, the mother's expression conveys anxiousness or fear (by frowning or opening her mouth slightly with the corners turned down), the baby infallibly turns around, seeks the haven of his mother's lap, and gives up his quest for the toy.

So the baby learns from his mother's face whether he is supposed to feel adventurous and brave, or fearful and defeatist. He simply attunes his state of mind (bravery or fear) to the expressions on his mother's face. This is a superb illustration of the way that the mother serves as a special kind of powerful mirror. The child will "learn" his state of emotions by reading the outward signs of it in his mother's face. He will make his mother's emotion his own by a kind of internalization that will determine his own emotional state as well as his actions. His decision to give up on a project or to stick it out will depend on the mother's approbation or fearfulness.

Emotional Referencing

It's not hard to imagine how important this phenomenon, which we call "emotional referencing," can be.

Again and again during the day, every time babies are faced with some new or ambiguous situation, they will find it necessary to scrutinize their mothers' faces. Robert Emde, a pioneer in research on emotional communication, has filmed the experiment I have just described, which he designed (Emde, Sorce 1983). Anyone who views this film will be struck by the automatic way the baby looks to his mother's expression and by the efficiency of the communication between them. Here is convincing proof of how closely babies are tuned in to their mothers, how precisely they react to messages from the mother. These take on the value of commands: "Keep going!" or else "Look out!"

Babies' dependence on their mothers has never been in doubt, but only recently has it become apparent that this dependency is not only a matter of satisfying basic needs for food, comfort, and affection. Babies are also emotionally dependent upon the mother's state of mind and are bound to shape their own inner states to fit hers.

Furthermore, babies' commitment to the world, their active engagement with their environment, also depend on the communications they receive from their mothers. Because this dependence is inevitable and unavoidable, I have taken to saying that babies are *under contract*. Short of becoming autistic, they have no choice but to take direction from their mothers' messages. When a mother signals the baby to do this or not to do that, he or she has to obey to maintain a relationship with the mother and respect the interactive convention laid down between them.

This emotional referencing that forms a sort of contract between baby and mother has many powerful effects. For one, babies are particularly sensitive to messages from the mother, especially messages with an emotional charge. This sensitivity allows the emotional state of the mother to influence the affective life of the baby. Maternal depression, for example, will have a direct effect on the baby. For this reason, when we seek to prevent or treat psychic problems in the baby, we do so *through the mother*. Babies are so tuned in to their mothers that a baby's emotional states can be modified by changing the mother's. This is why, in my work as an infant psychiatrist, I "treat" babies through the intermediary of their mothers.

The baby's sensitivity to the mother's messages is so great that, when the two are interacting, they may rightly be considered to be in a state of constant conversation. The vocabulary they use in this conversation is not made up of words but of facial expressions, voice inflections, and gestures, of moving closer and moving away. This vocabulary is much richer than may at first be imagined because it is put together in *sets*. The simultaneous occurrence of the elements I've just referred to (expressions, vocalization, gestures, and so on) have significance *together*. The confirmation of these elements conveys information, just as words do in ordinary language.

Within this signifying system, one other parameter is crucial—the time dimension. Because the expression-voice-gesture groupings come together in a reliable and preestablished sequence, they can take on a meaning. If, for example, the mother uses a certain expression after the baby has done a certain thing, then the baby will consider that sequence of events as a relation of cause and effect.

These messages set up by body language allow *psychological information* to be transmitted. By her movements, the mother "tells" her baby what she expects of him, what he can or cannot do, what gives her pleasure or pain. By internalizing these maternal messages, the baby will learn what he can share with his mother and what is taboo and will thereby force him into the loneliness of noncommunication. And it is by means of this internal representation that he will develop his self-image and move toward establishing himself as a person: "This is who I am!"

Years of research into this resonance and synchrony between mother and baby have made clear that babies can be understood only through careful scrutiny of their relations with their mothers. The famous English psychoanalyst D. W. Winnicott put it this way, in his book *The Child, the Family and the Outside World:* "A baby cannot exist alone, but is essentially part of a relation-ship."

The baby's joys and miseries can be grasped only if mother and baby are seen at the same time. Both mother and child have to be observed minutely as they interact, at the same time that careful attention is being paid to the themes that emerge from what the mother says about the child.

FOUR

A Thankless Role

*T*he glimpses in the previous chapter of the fascinating research on early interaction (Brazelton, Cramer 1990) help explain the puzzle we encountered earlier: how a baby learns to play his pre-ordained role in the scripts written by parents. This highly sensitive new being quickly learns to read the cues, to memorize his "lines" from the mother's voice, face, and gestures.

A Demand for Love

Let us return to Evelyn and Marie to see what lines Marie learned from her mother. Toward the middle of our first conversation, Evelyn Martin had switched from complaining about her daughter to complaining about her mother. She didn't see enough of her mother, and when she did get to see her she always had to share her mother with other people. Her resentment becomes more and more insistent as she speaks: she feels abandoned and deprived of affection.

At the very moment that Evelyn is revealing this demand for love, Marie, who is perched on her lap, drops her little shoe on the floor. Then she cries out, signaling to her mother that she should pick up the shoe for her. Evelyn refuses, quite peremptorily. Then Marie puts up her hand to touch her mother's face. Evelyn has an immediate reaction: "You almost scratched me then; I felt your nails."

She turns back to me and says, "She almost never shows me any sign of affection. . . . Sometimes, when you give someone a hug, you'd like to get one back . . . . [Turning to Marie] Don't scratch. . . . Give Mummy a little kiss." Then Marie signals that she wants to get down from her mother's knee, and Evelyn sets her on the floor. The sequence ends with distance put between them.

Now let's see how this scene can be deciphered, how the mother's state of mind can be linked to the interaction that produces the apparent symptom: scratching (i.e., the aggression that provokes the initial complaint).

First of all, what is the motivation behind the mother's behavior? What is the major theme that defines her relationship to her daughter and her mother? It is the demand for love, the feeling of being deprived of her mother. This is the essential theme running through the whole scene that has just been acted out and setting its tone. *Everything* that happens will be related to that search for love. When we focus this way, it is just as if we were seeing a film and using clues laid by the author in the first scenes to predict how each subsequent stage in the action will turn out.

It is precisely the moment when Evelyn is painfully evoking her mother's lack of attention that Marie chooses to demand Evelyn's attention. She has dropped her little boot (purposely?) and she complains, asking for her mother's help in getting it back—and her mother refuses.

Could it be that Evelyn Martin resents it when Marie begins to make demands of her at the very moment when she is stating *her own* demand for attention? She had wanted undivided attention from her mother; now she expects the same thing from me. She can no more bear it when Marie intervenes between us than when someone else gets in the way when she wants to be alone with her mother. Her refusal to respond to Marie's request is dictated by the demand she is making on the whole of my attention. I am now considered a stand-in for the mother, from whom everything is expected.

The interruption brought about by Marie's untimely demand will lead to an intensification of Evelyn's demand for love. This is now transferred once again, this time from the mother—who has failed to respond to her needs in the past—to Marie in the present. Evelyn accuses the child of not showing any affection. (But we know that right now Marie is being used as a double. Her refusal to kiss or hug her mother is resented only because she serves to recall a former longing for love that has been frustrated.)

In the grip of her own demand for love, Evelyn will "frustrate" Marie in turn, thereby reproducing quite unconsciously the original scene wherein a mother ignores her daughter's demands. Here before our eyes we can see how the exchanges between this mother and child act out a script of rejection that moves out of the past ("my mother rejected me when I was young") and into the present. An inner, private scenario becomes public.

Thus we arrive at a turning point, at a critical moment when the mother's subjective and inner drama shifts into an exchange acted out by two players. Marie puts her hand up to her mother's face, provoking the scratch sequence—"You are scratching me, . . . don't scratch"—then the mother pulls her face away.

In all probability, Marie had been feeling neglected when she asked her mother to pick up her shoe, and she had therefore tried harder to catch her attention, seeking bodily contact in a more insistent way, which Evelyn interpreted as aggressive. The speed with which Evelyn characterizes that action as aggressive suggests that she had foreseen that her child would respond in that way.

As chains of events of this sort happened several times, I decided that they indicated a model scenario that could be decoded in the following stages: Evelyn talks wistfully of her need for love. Marie seeks attention. Marie is frustrated. Marie makes her demand more insistently. Evelyn denounces her child's violence. Marie is put down.

Given the repetitive nature of these sequences, we can assume that there is a self-perpetuating mechanism at work, as if the two partners have agreed on their mutual goal. Marie is "under contract," bound to play her role: she has to starve her mother of affection, she has to hurt her.

The Child as a Screen

On the surface, the situation as I've just described it seems to make no sense. Why would a loving mother such as Evelyn want to induce her daughter to disappoint her and wound her? If Evelyn is expecting so much love from her daughter, why would she push her to act in precisely the opposite way?

What a strange contract this is in which the clauses all work against the interests of the person who drew it up! Yet such paradoxical contracts are not uncommon in human relationships. How many couples live lives together based on misunderstandings of this kind? How many married people relate to each other through quarrels and feed on mutual reproach? Some common and infernally efficient mechanism impels us to provoke other people into becoming the instruments of our own unhappiness.

Let me now suggest some reasons to explain why Evelyn would incite Marie to scratch her.

A baby has no words to plead her case. She is unable to answer, "But I didn't mean to scratch you. I was just trying to attract your attention, because you'd been talking to that gentleman for much too long." Her behavior can be interpreted in any number of ways. It can be read as saying what she really wanted to say, but her intentions can also be misinterpreted. According to her mood, the mother can read one of the baby's movements as a request for contact or as a mark of aggression.

Much more effectively than an older child who talks, a baby serves as a screen upon which her relatives can project various intentions.

We have a natural tendency to attribute to other people personal intentions of our own that we refuse to acknowledge because they are inconvenient or unsavory. Some other person is seen as the epitome or even the caricature of a trait that we prefer not to see in ourselves. Our own parents and our babies suffer particularly from this kind of projection. In most cases the assumption is that the baby is perfect. No evidence of this perfection is needed. The slightest little movement is called miraculous. When a little boy says his first words, he is already Lincoln reincarnate.

However, it is also possible to attribute all sorts of Machiavellian impulses to the baby. Howls are seen as a tyrant's commands, refusal to nurse is a challenge, a growing autonomy is an intolerable provocation.

In this way parents read complex meaning into their child's tiniest move, meanings that always provide crucial information about the hidden, unconscious intentions of the parents themselves. Nature has made it possible for us to understand our child only through the prism of our own inclinations. In fact it is by this process of attribution that we change this stranger, this newborn child, into a familiar being.

Erasing Old Sins

Early in our story, Evelyn had led us from Marie's aggressiveness to her mother's carpet-beater. She was rediscovering her mother through her daughter's abrupt gestures. The reason why she was so emphatic in seeing violence in gestures that seemed perfectly innocuous to an observer like myself was that she needed proof, evidence.

I then recalled another piece of data: at thirteen, Evelyn had slapped her mother. She spoke with great emotion of the mark her fingers had left on her mother's face. The guilt she felt had not lessened with time. In her opinion, it was unforgivable for a daughter to hit her mother.

Wasn't the litany of complaints about Marie's violence a way of expressing her old feeling of being responsible? Marie became the screen on which she projected the violence she had once unleashed. Her own cheek was now intended to bear the mark of Marie's scratching fingers just as her mother's face had once borne the mark of her own hand.

It now seemed that she was asking Marie to mark her face so that in her turn she could be the victim of her daughter's excesses. By leading Marie to strike her she sought to erase the mark of her fingers on her own mother's face.

The roles have been reversed. Evelyn has gotten into her mother's skin and she expects Marie to play her own role of rebellious daughter.

This is the price Evelyn feels obliged to pay if she hopes to erase the mark of her old guilt. She must suffer at the hands of her daughter to win forgiveness from her mother.

This whole scenario serves several purposes. Marie has to scratch her mother so that Evelyn can be freed from an old weight of guilt. But, at the same time, dissension has to be set up between mother and daughter because this is what Evelyn was familiar with in her relations with her mother. And all this is facilitated by my presence: Evelyn ignores Marie's request for attention because she needs to have my exclusive attention so that I can witness her suffering.

Even when this threefold scenario has been interpreted, the situation is far from exhausted. Other critical elements lie even deeper and emerge only in later sessions. But, as a first stage, this degree of interpretation was already enough to alter the situation. The father's part in all this was also to emerge later, as we shall see further on in this book.

FIVE

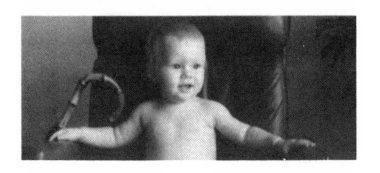

❦

Whose Symptoms?

*A*s the head of a child psychiatry unit in a teaching hospital that is willing to explore any therapeutic approach to the problem of disturbed children, I continually run up against the following problem. What form of therapy is indicated when the roots of the disorder lie not only with the designated patient (the child) but also with another person (the parent)? As every practicing child psychiatrist has occasion to note, even when the child is the one with the symptoms, the cure often lies with the parents. This is quite clear in the case of Marie and Evelyn. This does not mean that the parents are *the* cause of the problem; the child (and the course of events) also play a part. However, very often it turns out that a problem has been triggered and nourished by the parents' conflicts, anxieties, and fantasies.

In any case, it is unproductive to look for a single cause, one isolated pathogenic agent, responsible for the

whole problem. As in the field of immunology, we must
think in terms of circuits and systems. An outside force
is a threat only if it corresponds to a vulnerability in the
subject: a circuit is arranged between external causes
and internal characteristics. The particular conflicts or
emotions experienced by the parents will give rise to
symptoms in the child only if that child is biopsycholog-
ically receptive to that influence. And a given trait in the
child's character will upset the dialogue with the parents
only if it serves to destabilize their defense mechanisms.

The outbreak of symptoms does not depend on
isolated factors but on the way those factors happen to
affect the parent-child exchange. For this reason, it is
the parent-child relationship that must be "treated"
first.

Yet all too often the parents who bring us "problem children" are not ready or willing to be considered
as patients. Parents frequently protest, saying, "We
came here because our son has a problem and here you
are psychoanalyzing us!" The psychiatrist has to respect
these resistances, which often signal a real weakness or
else an excessive fear of being criticized or exposed.

The best strategy in such cases is to set up a series
of "consultations" with the parents first, and then with
the child. In this way, without putting the parents off
their balance, certain misunderstandings and short
circuits that are destroying the relationship can be
corrected. Such relatively brief meetings of this sort

are well tolerated by parents, and not infrequently a new relationship is set up. Then, if the child's symptoms are not alleviated, more prolonged and thorough therapy may be proposed.

With infants, the need to involve parents is clearer. Even if it is the baby who "has" the symptoms, it is always the relationship that must be treated, because the baby alone cannot become a therapeutic partner. In most cases, moreover, psychotherapeutic modifications in the parents lead to a rapid change in the interaction, and thus to a simultaneous improvement in the child. In adopting this approach, our assumption, or wager, is that it is the relationship which is pathological and which must be treated therapeutically. And since, in any case, the mother's conflicts and fantasies mold her dialogue with her baby (whether pathological or not), it is to the mother that the interpretations will be addressed. These interpretations will focus on those conflicts, fantasies, and anxieties that are bound up with her status as a mother, with her relation to the child, and with whatever is pathological in the child's response (that is, the child's symptoms).

The Infant's Role in Therapy

Even though it is the mother's psyche that determines the pathological scenarios of the interaction, this does not mean that we can simply treat *her* as the patient and limit the treatment to *her* problems. In fact, treatment of a mother on her own and of a mother with her baby is completely different. Experience proves that the presence of the baby plays a crucial role. During the sessions, babies engage their mothers by their attitudes and behavior. In this way they powerfully mobilize their mothers' thoughts and emotions.

A mother will react to a baby's activity with comments that reveal the link to her own problems. She also reacts with motions and gestures that can be linked to what she is saying. Thus the baby plays a revelatory and catalytic role. Without the baby's presence, the psychiatrist lacks an indispensable aid; the interactions reveal crucial information.

When the baby is there, the psychiatrist watches a whole relationship develop before his or her eyes and can link it immediately to what the mother is revealing, both verbally and in her reactions, about herself, her past, her relation to her baby. Often the baby acts out in vivid behavior the fantasy that the mother has just put into words.

Both research and treatment are focused on this conjunction of what is happening (the interaction) and what is being said (the verbal report). This "bifocal" approach, which I have described in detail in an earlier book written with the pediatrician T. Berry Brazelton, is essential in the psychotherapy of mother and baby. It allows us to see clearly how the contents of the mother's psyche are expressed in interactive behavior. It also offers proof of the basic hypothesis behind infant psychiatry and this book: that disturbed behavior in an infant can be changed by bringing about intrapsychic transformations in the mother.

What about Fathers?

I shall be returning later to the place of the father in the parent-child relationship. For the moment, in this rapid summary of the nature of my therapeutic practice, let me say just one thing. In the majority of cases, it is the mother who requests a consultation, and she is the one who feels most involved.

When a mother requests a consultation, it usually means that, however unconsciously, she realizes that her anguish is the issue, and that behind the problems she is having with her child are hidden other problems relating to her own history. Proof that this is so comes when, in the course of the early sessions, the mother changes her focus and associates her worries about the child with earlier conflicts in her life. As we saw with Evelyn Martin, behind the child loomed the figure of Evelyn's own mother.

Most frequently, the mother will choose to undertake a process of discovery in which she takes on the status of a patient. My feeling is that, since it is she who requests the consultation, the mother has a right to explore these personal realms with a guarantee of professional confidentiality and to feel secure in what we call a "privileged relationship" with the therapist.

If the husband were brought in, a whole new dynamic would develop that might impede the process of self-discovery so often found in mother-baby therapy. In classic psychotherapy, of course, there would be no question of insisting upon the participation of the spouse.

All the same, there are cases when both parents ask to come to the sessions, and this can also lead to productive therapy.

The "Cruel" Child: A Study in Transformation

How is it possible to demonstrate "objectively" that a link exists between the psychic modifications a mother experiences in the course of therapy and the consequent changes in her relationship with her baby?

In order to study this, my colleague Daniel Stern

applied a "microanalytic" technique to interactions that I had previously recorded during a brief psychotherapy of a mother and baby. ("Evaluation of Changes in Mother-Infant Brief Psychotherapy: A Single Case Study," *Infant Mental Health Journal,* Vol. 9, No. 1, Spring 1988). This project involved a great deal of work. Five hours of video recording had to be carefully studied while the interactive behaviors of which we were seeking objective evidence were identified and then counted. Then it was necessary to establish the correlations between the child's solicitations and the mother's responses, and vice versa. Finally, the incidence of these interactions had to be shown in the form of a graph, so that interactions from the beginning and from the end of the treatment could be compared.

The case in question had many similarities to that of Evelyn and Marie.

A young mother was complaining about the behavior of her son Sebastian, ten months old, claiming that he showed her no affection and refused to be held. The mother was so anxious that she had been asking her pediatrician for help several times a month, either because Sebastian wasn't sleeping or because he would start screaming with pain and distress for no obvious organic reason.

From our very first meeting, the mother described

Sebastian as a little monster and accused him of taking pleasure in hurting her. An example of the way she would attribute cruelty to her baby occurred before my eyes: Just as she was telling me about the pain the child had caused during pregnancy and labor, Sebastian began to rock to and fro, hitting his mother hard in the chest. I was struck by the coincidence between the mother's statement and the way it was borne out in their interaction. I was forced to conclude that the mother, in some way, needed to show me that she was the victim of a destructive baby. I hypothesized that there was some subtle mechanism whereby these painful interactions were induced, but I could not spot it. The longer we continued, the surer I was that Sebastian was "under contract" to torture his mother. Later sessions provided me with the basic elements of this scenario, and through microanalysis the hidden mechanism of the interaction was revealed.

The Central Scenario

Once again I was profoundly impressed by the parallels between this mother's psychic problems and the characteristic way in which she behaved with her son. Her problems were the result of a long history of hospitalizations and illnesses. The self-image she had progressively developed was marked by a feeling of great physical vulnerability. She always felt she was in danger and feared being injured or scarred. In the course of her numerous illnesses, which had begun in childhood, she had been given up for dead several times. Her youth had been sadly marked by operations and bodily pain. Suffering seemed to be her lot in life and now, all of a sudden, the assaults on her body that she had suffered in the past were being repeated, through Sebastian. He had caused her pain during the pregnancy, had forced her to endure a cesarean, had pulled out the intravenous line attached to her arm just after his birth, had been rough when she was nursing him, now he was hitting her, and so on.

There seemed to be no end to this long list of sufferings. Inevitably, Sebastian would be forced into the role of torturer—forced, as it were, to continue a tradition of suffering.

The interactions between mother and baby appeared to confirm such a prediction. It seemed inevitable that everything would conspire to inflict painful encounters on this woman.

The central scenario is thus one of someone forcefully inflicting pain on a woman's body. In the past it had been the surgeons who did violence to her body. From now on it would be Sebastian. Bodily contact of any sort provoked such anxiety in this mother that she had no longer tolerated sexual intercourse since Sebastian's birth.

The Goal of Therapy

More than one problem was involved here:

- The mother anticipated that Sebastian would attack her violently, as others had done in her painful past.
- At the same time, she was provoking Sebastian into a state of hyperactivity, using him to lift herself brutally out of her habitual state of passivity and torpor. Her father had been compelled to jostle her roughly in this way all through her childhood.
- Finally, it seemed that she was projecting onto Sebastian a violent hatred she could not keep to herself and of which her parents were the real target.

The goal of therapy was to allow this mother to decontaminate a present relation from the violence that belonged to the past. In this way she could come to see Sebastian with new eyes, without projecting onto him the violence that made her fear all physical contact. In therapy, this mother also learned to handle her own depressive passivity, to let herself be, and thus stop using Sebastian and his assumed hyperactivity as a means of "waking her up." As the therapy progressed, the interactions became less aggressive. By our fourth session, Sebastian even managed to fall asleep in his mother's arms, much to her amazement.

Watching for Change

In order to identify and quantify changes in mother and baby during therapy, we studied and recorded each of the mother's responses to Sebastian's "aggressive" acts. As the treatment went on, she became much more sensitive to his gestures. In fact her ability to react increased spectacularly from 0 percent to 75 percent at the time of interactions. This ability led moreover to a particular kind of interaction: Whereas at the beginning the mother tried to ignore Sebastian's "aggressions," as our sessions continued, she began to respond to them and transform them into a kind of game. She seemed to have understood that the baby was asking her things and trying to communicate and that she was supposed to respond.

By studying these reactions in detail, we discovered that what was increasing was the mother's ability to transform the aggressions into positive communications. During the same period her reactions of avoidance and rejection decreased just as spectacularly (from 70 percent of the interactions in the beginning to 3 percent at the end of the treatment).

What happened? The attribution of aggression to the child was modified. The mother managed to relegate her own experience of violence to her past and, from this point on, she interpreted Sebastian's "aggressions" not as an intent to harm her but as a desire for contact. Her attitudes, and therefore her behavior, were transformed. Once she had avoided Sebastian's advances and showed no awareness of what could be called his "appeals," but now she was able to see them as a way of communicating. As a result, the atmosphere of their interactions had profoundly changed.

This transformation was apparent on other levels. In the beginning, Sebastian spent 25 percent of the time on his mother's knee; by the end, this mode of contact had increased to 76 percent of the time. In the same way, whereas at the beginning the child and the mother never positioned themselves face to face, this mode of contact had multiplied eightfold by the end of the treatment.

We also observed a massive increase in exchanges of affection and moments of affective attunement, that is, of exchanges demonstrating a reciprocal understanding.

Our quantitative study allowed us to confirm that changes in the mother's psyche had led to changes in the mother-baby relations. Moreover, the microanalysis helped us to understand the symptom: Sebastian's aggressive agitation. We could see that at the beginning the mother's only reaction to Sebastian's aggressions was evasion. You could say that this was a case where reciprocity had broken down: the mother was refusing to respond and attend to the child because she thought he was aggressive.

Once she was able to modify her interpretation of Sebastian's behavior, she started to respond to her son. A new language developed, facilitating exchanges and giving satisfaction to both partners. Once mother and son had been deaf to each other's messages, but now a harmonious conversation had been established. Sebastian's aggression can thus be understood to arise from an intensification of demands to which his mother did not reply.

Our study demonstrated that crucial changes in interaction between mother and baby can take place when the mother's mental representations are transformed by psychotherapy.

When this mother realized that she was projecting upon Sebastian an intent to do violence, and that at the same time she was expecting him to stimulate her by his abrupt movements, her image of the child changed. This transformation of the child's image in turn eased her anxiety. She no longer feared that Sebastian would cause her pain.

Words were able to open the door into the elusive world of fantasies, anxieties, and memories, thereby bringing about a change that broke the vicious cycle of imagined violence made actual. A purely psychic modification revolutionized the nature of the daily encounters between Sebastian and his mother.

These transformations in the mother-child relationship were due to the effects of psychotherapy on the maternal psyche. The baby was changed by this process, showing that the mother's unconscious marks the child's psyche.

The passage from fantasy to the reality of mother-infant relations was the object of our study, confirming that feelings, ideas, and the content of the psyche can set their seal on behavior, and that this phenomenon can be studied objectively. The quantitative nature of this research is indispensable if we wish to maintain that psychotherapy works and can be worthy of scientific inquiry.

This change from mental images to observable behavior, this passage from a psychic into a material realm, reveals how the maternal unconscious is communicated to the baby. By their gestures toward their babies, mothers have throughout the ages transmitted what they expected and what the babies were to think of themselves. This is how the transmission of a psychological heritage from generation to generation takes place.

SIX

Why Do We Make Babies?

❧

*O*n one occasion the
pediatric clinic at our hospital called me about an emergency situation. Celine, a baby girl four months old, was systematically refusing to eat. She had been admitted to the hospital because she could not get above her birth weight. Even in the hospital things did not improve, and the pediatricians had been obliged to feed her intravenously. An even more disturbing fact was that the baby's condition got worse when her mother was present. When she held Celine, the mother's nervousness was transmitted to the baby, who started struggling and throwing up. Mrs. Girard believed she was doing the right thing. Every time Celine woke up or made a sound, a bottle was put into her mouth. Mrs. Girard explained to me, "At home I have a full bottle ready in every room in the house. As soon as Celine opens her eyes, I give her her bottle!"

This forced feeding was only one part of the

mother's hyperactive behavior. She talked nonstop, addressing an uninterrupted stream of questions at the baby, and seeking to attract her attention by boisterous games. Faced with this intolerable barrage, Celine had developed an effective strategy. At the mere sight of her mother waving a feeding bottle, she fell asleep, so soundly that no stimulus could wake her up!

Taking refuge in sleep was the baby's only defense against her mother's repeated intrusions.

To observe such scenes of the mother's misplaced insistence and Celine's systematic retreat was to see a tragic illustration of a relationship that had reached a serious impasse. These partners had reached a point of no return; an encounter between them set up no reciprocal dialogue. Each was captive to her own urgent needs and demands. At the hospital, we were all horror-stricken to see that disharmony with her mother had led this baby to act in a way that threatened her survival.

Ghosts at the Cradle

Mrs. Girard was very worried about Celine's health. In our talks, she started to talk about her past, and about recent deaths that had gravely upset her. As a small child, she had been abandoned by her parents and been raised by her grandmother and an uncle. This couple had become parental substitutes.

Two years after her grandmother's death, her uncle had developed cancer. It was during that illness that Mrs. Girard conceived Celine. During her pregnancy she was grief-stricken to see the swift deterioration of her uncle's health and his loss of weight. He was no longer able to eat.

The coincidence between the uncle's last illness and the pregnancy, between the dying man's alimentary problems and Celine's, indicated that there was some link between the sufferings of these two. Celine was now trapped by the anxious terror Mrs. Girard had felt for her uncle. Once I had established this link between daughter and uncle, the mother confessed to me that she was convinced that Celine was also suffering from a fatal form of cancer.

This intense conviction worried me. Mrs. Girard acted as if Celine *was* her uncle, slowly dying before her very eyes, just as her uncle had done.

One person was being mistaken for another, this was all too clear, and the mother had lost her powers of judgment. We were witnessing a projection of a particularly malignant form, already invading the flesh of this little baby who was unable to gain weight.

We were now in a better position to understand the mother's extreme agitation and her attempts to force milk down the baby's throat. She was struggling as best she could against the child's death sentence. Before she could calm down, she needed to realize the confusion in her mind between the dead uncle and Celine, and to undertake the neglected task of mourning for her uncle. Once this occurred, the baby's anorexia began to disappear rapidly.

Mourning and Birth

Celine had been conceived while her mother was suffering through the death of her uncle, her last relative. It seems safe to suggest that Celine was conceived to keep an irremediable loss at bay, to "replace" the person who was dying.

I made this interpretation fairly confidently, since clinical practice has taught me how common this replacement mechanism is.

Our instinct to reproduce is also an instinct to rediscover. We are not simply reproducing *ourselves* but also our ancestors. There is a cycle of loss and creation. A child is a link with the past and carries the promise that we will find again what has gone. Children help us forget the loss of old relationships and are born "under contract" to revive those whom we loved and lost. For these reasons it is not surprising that the wish for a child is often strengthened and sharpened following a death in the family.

The Replacement Child

There are many examples of children being born immediately after a family has gone into mourning. Salvador Dalí, for example, was well aware that he was replacing another little Salvador, who had died as a child. He has told us that acting extremely oddly was his way of emphasizing his presence, and thus counteracting the constant threat posed by the stronger presence of his dead brother. The bravura of his behavior served to annihilate the other's presence and exorcise his death anxieties.

Vincent van Gogh was born one year after the early death of another Vincent. Every morning, when he left his father's rectory, he passed the cemetery where he could read his own name on a tomb. How hard it must be to know one's fate is to replace another person! How difficult for the child whose task is to erase the memory of another before he himself is accepted as a person. This task is made all the more difficult by the way that we view children who die young as perfect beings, since they have no time to disappoint their relatives. It is no easy task to live up to the ideal portrait of a dead brother.

The Burden of Names

Freud used to say that we turn our children into ghosts through the names we give them. In choosing a name, we also choose a destiny. It's not easy to be called Napoleon or Jesus or even to learn that the name we bear casts us in the image of some dead grandparent.

The choice of a given name always says something about family tradition, about a link through the child that more or less secretly binds the parent to an ideal image. In many traditional societies, children always bear the first name of an ancestor, either that of the deceased grandparent or a fetish name that recalls some famous ancestor or someone who bears a special aura.

On one occasion, a young mother, Mrs. C., brought her eleven-month-old twins to see me. She was worried about the male twin. He was less advanced than his sister, slower in learning to sit up alone, and seemed physically more fragile. He was also much shyer than his sister and less assertive. When the twins competed, the sister usually won.

Mrs. C. was notably intelligent and very tuned in to psychic realities. In our talks, it was she who spontaneously made the crucial association. The twins were conceived in the days just following the sudden death of their paternal grandfather, a death that had deeply affected her whole family. As she told me this, she went on without pause to explain that the baby boy's name means "my father is gentle" in the family's native language. Thus it was clear that the grandfather's shadow loomed over the boy who was intended to make up the loss. At first sight, this looked like a typical replacement scenario. However, in this case as in so many others, I had to bow before the infinite richness presiding over children's destinies. Just like a Russian doll, this first theme of mourning opened up to reveal others.

Mrs. C. had also been a twin. Her brother had died suddenly from a rare illness. There were therefore two male deaths to confront, and, by a trick of fate that we often find in our consultations, this double sorrow had been laid upon a destiny already unusually weighed down by tragic loss. Several of the men in the family had lost their lives in wartime.

Mrs. C.'s concern was all too understandable. Was her son to inherit the terrible fate of early death that marked the men in the family, but not the women? When she saw that her son was less sturdy than her daughter, it was natural for her to imagine that he carried the family weakness since she also had been stronger than her twin brother.

The fact that he had been conceived in an atmosphere of mourning and that his name served to commemorate a newly dead relative, the coincidence between death and birth, all made it easy for her to

associate or even identify the baby with his vanished
"ancestors."

This whole scenario of commemorations and
gloomy predictions needed to be brought into the light
in order to exorcise the specter of a weak and doomed
existence. In the process, Mrs. C.'s astonishing ability
to establish psychological links and use them to change
her attitudes provided the essential dynamics of the
treatment. She was intensely reassured when her son
began to hold his own against his sister. This new stur-
diness was in great part acquired because Mrs. C.
stopped trying, selectively, to protect her son from his
sister. At the beginning, she used to take him in her
arms every time there was a dispute. By setting up this
kind of reaction, she was transmitting to her son the
notion of his own vulnerability. As soon as she allowed
him to stand up for himself without running to his
rescue, he emerged from his passivity and became his
sister's equal.

Psychological Heredity

This phenomenon of replacement reveals a remarkable
fidelity to its original models. We all carry within us
images of parents and other relatives on whom we
model ourselves and with whom we keep up a dialogue,
however imaginary, that is charged with values and

emotions. This is how a permanent family tradition is maintained. Our ancestors' psychology is transmitted from generation to generation, making each of us a link in a long chain.

Heredity is not only passed on through genes. It is inscribed in the messages that each parent necessarily transmits to each child. We must all deal with the fact that the wish for a child, in ourselves or our parents, serves to make up for losses and to recapture old relationships.

Even if a child is not conceived immediately following the death of a particular relative, he or she represents a chance to make up for the loss of childhood relationships. We are all nostalgic for our early childhood, and each child offers a promise of finding the essence of that childhood once again.

The Child as Healer

If children are born as replacements, they will be expected to cure their parents of nostalgia. They are intended to restore in full what we feel as an empty longing.

Birth will conceal death; new life will erase loss.

Hence the newborn child is meant to make up for disappointments that the parents never managed to overcome by other means. Seen in this way, it is easy to understand the intensity of the demands made upon a baby—and the enormity of the task laid upon him or her. How can a baby respond to expectations that date back to the parents' own childhoods? How can the child incarnate a person whom the parents have not adequately mourned?

Eastern religions are not alone in preaching the doctrine of reincarnation. Many of the people we run into every day may start to believe in reincarnation once they have a baby.

Mrs. Jordan came for a consultation because she was very upset by the constant crying of her ten-week-old daughter, Nora. She immediately began describing an incident when her child stopped breathing because she was crying so hard. Mrs. Jordan had been panic-stricken when this happened and since then had been putting Nora constantly to the breast to prevent her from getting upset. She was afraid that the baby would suffer respiratory arrest and die. At the same time, as happens so often in cases of intense anxiety, her milk had dried up.

This scenario of anxiety and tense relations between mother and baby soon switched to another scene with a common theme: preoccupation with death. Mrs. Jordan spoke with great emotion of the sudden and unexplained death of her maternal grandmother four years earlier. This unexpected loss had thrown her completely off balance. She had never recovered and had dreamed about her grandmother every night for six months. Her maternal aunt had been so much affected by the death that she had consulted a medium and had been drawn heavily into spiritualism. When Mrs. Jordan had told her aunt of her pregnancy, the aunt had replied, "I know through my medium that the baby will be a girl," and she assured her niece that the child would be the reincarnation of her great-grandmother.

Mrs. Jordan paused at this point, telling me she didn't have much faith in spirits. At the same time she asked me if I believed in reincarnation and told me a story that has greatly alarmed her. Right after her grandmother's death, she had dug up a primrose plant from her grandmother's rock garden and replanted it in her own garden. During the three years following the grandmother's death, the plant bore no flowers, but it bloomed quite suddenly the week before Nora's birth.

For Mrs. Jordan, the flowering was a sign of return to life, and its coincidence with Nora's birth indicated to her that her grandmother had chosen the child for her reincarnation. Since that time, she was always on the lookout for any little thing to prove that her intuition was correct. Thus she noted that Nora's eyes were blue, "just like my grandmother's," and, to confirm this filiation, she had given Nora her grandmother's name as a second name.

In the same breath that Mrs. Jordan was providing

me with these "proofs" that her grandmother had been reproduced in her daughter, she also announced that she dared not *really* believe in reincarnation as it would be much too scary.

Her fear was quite understandable, I told her. She was "confusing" her daughter and her grandmother to such an extent that she expected Nora to suffer respiratory arrest at any moment and die just as her grandmother had done.

As we might have expected, Mrs. Jordan had been very close to her grandmother, whereas she had known nothing but conflict and disappointment with her mother.

In the course of therapy, Mrs. Jordan and I managed to establish that she had reincarnated her grandmother in her daughter out of a desire to re-create the "idyllic" relationship she remembered with that grandmother. Worries had arisen as the image of her own mother crept into the ideal relationship, haunting the bond of love like a jealous Fury.

The Power of Reincarnation

The phenomenon of reincarnation is thus double-edged. It allows us to reunite with a loved one whom we have lost and who takes on the image of the newborn child.

The parent will thus see the features of the loved object in the face and actions of the baby.

But reincarnation is also unsettling; the shadow of the dead person who is returning to life looms disconcertingly. When a dead person leans over the crib, the visit threatens to be alarming. In fact if the loved one has been idealized, he or she can quickly turn into a dread ghost. Malignant images often lurk behind the faces we love to conjure up from the past, so often is it that the beloved contains its evil opposite.

In just this way, the grandmother's loving blue eyes had found new life in Nora, but so had the mother's look of hate.

The theme of reincarnation is actually very common. In most cases, the link with an "ancestor" is represented in a discreet and symbolic fashion—by preserving a first name, by seeing some common character trait. Every child, as we have seen, represents someone else. But when belief in reincarnation turns into certainty, the parent ceases to be able to distinguish between the child and the dead relative. The baby *is* the grandmother.

When a ghost takes over a newborn baby in this way, an entire lifetime can be shaped according to a borrowed identity. Everyone will deal with the child as if he or she were someone else. All the feelings that had bound the parents to the original object are now

carried over onto the child whose fate it is to be someone else. "I am an other," as Rimbaud said. It cannot
be easy to become oneself while being someone else,
and the only way to prevent a child from incurring
such a hard fate is to exorcise the unconscious
phantom.

Mrs. Jordan told me during our second conversation that she had had a dream. She could see her grandmother, much more beautiful than in reality, in an
exceptionally luxurious house, saying to her, "You must
forget me now." It was a good dream, she told me.
Mrs. Jordan felt better and worried less about Nora
once she realized that she had carried over onto her
child all the anxieties associated with her grandmother's
death.

Following the dream of her grandmother, Mrs.
Jordan talked at length about her parents and the disappointments they had caused her. We were able to understand that it was her disillusionment with her parents
that had led her to idealize her grandmother (whose
beauty and domestic luxury were exaggerated in the
dream).

Once she had come to understand these feelings,
Mrs. Jordan finally felt free after four years to mourn
her grandmother instead of holding her suspended in a
kind of half-life. This process freed Nora in turn from
the presence of an eerie phantom. There is a good

chance that we were thus able to change the course of a destiny by exorcising an unwanted third person.

The Tiny Magician

We often hear in fairy stories about good fairies who bestow magic gifts upon newborn children. Then the wicked fairy arrives, defies the protective spirits, and tries to take over the baby's fate. All cradles are surrounded with such invisible presences who conjure up amazing phenomena as if by magic.

In most cases, the baby turns into a magician. Babies are believed to have amazing talents, and they actually do have great powers. When a newborn comes into the world, parents undergo a radical shift in behavior, transform their entire way of life, and make this little being the center of their world. The baby is a conjurer.

There's something about the arrival of a baby that makes such magic possible. It is as if the birth enabled the parents to reenter the magic realms of their childhoods. In these realms, magical thinking prevails, a belief in the impossible. The child's wishes become reality and the limitations of the real world are ignored. The baby's coming offers the illusion that, once again, all things are possible. Love will be perfect. The craziest plans take on new life.

Black Magic

Sometimes, however, babies deal in black magic. Their powers, far from being beneficent, bring bad times, and parents see them as evil spirits.

Mrs. Morgan and her daughter Vanessa have been referred to me by her pediatrician. Vanessa, aged ten months, has two symptoms: she doesn't eat and is very agitated. Mealtimes have turned into battles, and Mrs. Morgan remembers that, until the age of ten, she too had fought her mother constantly during meals.

Vanessa is seen as a "bad girl": her mother says, "She takes all the good out of me." Vanessa is also extremely rebellious and turns "purple with rage" when she is restrained. Mrs. Morgan goes on to say that she also had been unable to bear her own alcoholic father's outbursts of anger.

In the course of our conversations, I am struck by how hyperactive Vanessa is. I can see how easy it would be to see her as demonic. It's at this point that Mrs. Morgan dares to ask me if I can explain some dreams. During her pregnancy, she had dreamt that people were saying that her fetus was the devil. This had upset her very much and reminded her of two memories she had retained from seeing the movie *The Exorcist*. Everything was constantly in motion, and a little girl (the heroine of the movie) was speaking with a man's voice. There followed a description of Mrs. Morgan's younger brother, of whom she had been very jealous, and who "turned out badly," ending up as a patient in a psychiatric hospital.

Since Vanessa's birth, this demonic image, associated with madness, had in the mother's view been coming true. First of all, Vanessa was in constant motion and then, since she was already able to "play games" at five months, Mrs. Morgan was convinced the child was possessed.

Whose spirit could be possessing this tiny baby? Whose ghost was she? Gradually it turned out that Mrs. Morgan had projected onto Vanessa a complex composite image: her reincarnated father the alcoholic and her brother the madman, as well as her own long history of vigorous rebellion against her parents.

In the course of our conversations, Vanessa calmed down a lot, but Mrs. Morgan proved quite unable to change the bad opinion she had of her daughter. My therapy had little effect on the diabolic projection she had made. This mother could not manage to clear her child of evil intent and continued to have recourse to magical thinking. In fact, she started to study the tarot, announcing that "she was doing a lot of work on Ika, the devil's card"! Black magic had won the day.

The Value of the Postpartum Crisis

About the third or fourth day after giving birth, many new mothers are seized by an unexpected fit of the blues or weep very easily. In some cases this will be followed by a progressive sense of depression.

Important hormonal changes occur in the days following a birth: estrogen levels fall with the shedding of the placenta, and there is an increase in the secretion of prolactin, the hormone that triggers milk production. In addition to these changes, the body shape is transformed. The pregnant woman's large, tight, round belly suddenly becomes flabby and empty.

Any rapid and irreversible physical change can trigger a psychological crisis. Such a crisis is all the more likely when the image and perception of the body have been upset.

On the psychological level, important modifications have been in the works throughout the nine months of pregnancy. Parents have been forced to accept the pregnancy's reality by observing the changes in the mother's body and by watching the images of the baby on the ultrasound monitor. They are obliged to adapt progressively to the idea that they are no longer children but parents. This shift entails a revaluation of their relations with their own parents, with whom they now find themselves on an equal footing. Old issues of rivalry are revived. Progressively, the parents identify themselves with their own parents.

At the same time, one can observe in mothers re-emerging images of their own childhood relationships to their mothers. This leads to childish desires, and the pregnant woman may even begin to identify with the baby about to be born.

Thus a kind of oscillation is set up between two opposite and complementary identifications. It is as if the mother-to-be were "trying out" her role as a mother, while at the same time imagining what it is like to be a baby. This is a critically important process since it allows the mother to dream of the future (the coming of the baby) while reliving her past (the relation she had as a baby to her mother). She prepares herself by remembering.

This oscillation of alternative identifications occurs unconsciously, but it is a very important factor in analysis with pregnant women. The analytic situation makes it clear that an upheaval in the psychic self-image is taking place, forcing the mother to "review" the identity she had forged for herself. This does not happen painlessly, and the mother will need psychological support from outside, whether from her family (her husband and her mother) or from professionals (doctors, midwives, and others).

This threat to the self-image leads to a psychological crisis. The advantage of this "crisis" is that it helps prepare the way for the newborn. The mother gains access to parts of her unconscious that had remained latent, hidden. Her imaginative capacity is thereby enriched. As a result, the mother becomes much more receptive, much more sensitive, more open to the demands that her encounter with the new child will make on her.

At the same time, pregnant women experience swift mood swings, and thoughts long been held at bay come to the surface. A birth turns everything topsy-turvy and makes a woman particularly receptive to what is happening in her psyche. Pregnancy and birth make women particularly amenable to therapeutic intervention. From the point of view of a psychiatrist, this period is a "privileged moment" for preventive psychotherapy.

The Sadness of Birth

Birth itself is a shock—a biological shock in the first place, but then a psychic shock also. The mother has to face the loss of a part of herself (the empty womb), and, curiously, the baby's actual presence does not always fill the gap. Many mothers remember their pregnancy as a blessed time, a high point in their feeling of fulfillment. They felt in top shape. Chronic symptoms sometimes disappear; often women feel euphoric. (Of course there are also pregnancies that go badly, filled with vomiting, weariness, all kinds of anxiety, but such cases are less common.)

After this period of fulfillment, it is often difficult to adapt to the sudden change of the birth, and a feeling of loss may prevail.

This feeling of loss contributes to the sadness that many mothers experience in the days after the birth. Sometimes women sink into a true clinical depression.

A patient of mine, Mrs. Suarez, suffered exactly this kind of postpartum depression. She was forced to take medication as she was feeling so low. Her third child, a darling little girl named Maria, had been born six months earlier, and yet she explained to me pathetically that she could not play with the baby. She felt detached and dreamed of going away somewhere.

What country was she dreaming of, I asked. What was she homesick for? She then explained that she had been born some time after the sudden death of a brother in an accident, and that throughout her childhood she had suffered because she could not lessen her parents' sadness.

Little by little we approached the question of whether she regretted having been born, since birth established her irretrievable difference from her brother, who could never be dethroned from his parents' affection.

At the deepest point in her depression, when she

was weeping by Maria's side, Mrs. Suarez told me why she was so homesick. She could not play with Maria because the baby was outside her body. She sobbed as she said, "I want her to still be inside me." Her longing to be permanently pregnant was the equivalent of her longing for her mother's womb. *To have* a baby (in her womb) gave her the illusion of *being* the baby (in her mother's womb).

In her pregnancies she was trying to do away with separation, with the loss of the fetus's union with the mother. Her nostalgia was so strong that the anatomical separation of birth had become intolerable to her, hence her depression. Maria, there, in front of her, was the painful reminder of her own exclusion.

As I watched Mrs. Suarez and Maria side by side, the mother weeping and the daughter watching her in silence, I noted that Maria paid particular attention to her mother's face and scrutinized it with special intensity when her mother was weeping hardest. Was she trying to distract her mother just as the latter had tried to make her own parents forget the loss they had suffered?

Mrs. Suarez confirmed that I was right and, some months later, she reported that her daughter made constant efforts to comfort her. But Maria did not succeed in cheering her mother up. She too failed in her attempts to modify, by loving care, her mother's sadness. She in her turn was experiencing the same despair that her mother felt when she had sought to compensate for the loss of her brother. Without realizing it, Mrs. Suarez was making her daughter experience the same sense of impotence that had weighed on her own childhood.

Enter the Real Child

The real baby will never correspond to the imaginary baby. A gap opens up as soon as the cord is cut. And that gap will be filled with whatever parents and children can build together. Otherwise it will remain a chasm, a wound that scars every relationship in the future with shared disillusion.

Into this gap vanish the parents' projections, as they stubbornly try to reduce the difference, to force the child to fit the model.

Children react differently to the force of these projections. Sometimes they react vigorously, refusing to conform to any constraint. Sometimes, on the contrary, they go along with parental expectations and accommodate them as best they can. All kinds of compromises emerge. One thing remains unexplained, however—why certain children offer far greater immunity than others to their parents' script. They somehow play their parts without losing a sense of self. In such cases there is a kind of alchemy at work between the parental desires and the way the child deals with them. This alchemy plays a central part in the success or failure of the relationship between parents and children.

In this alchemy, the baby's own characteristics will play a crucial role. As we now know, the newborn child is not a wax tablet on which the parents can write at will. Babies also shape their partners and construct their own experience.

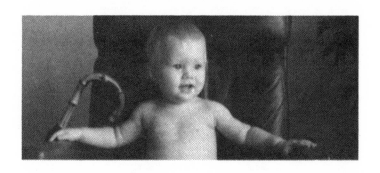

SEVEN

How Babies Rewrite the Script

*T*he reader who has followed me this far is probably surprised that my account of the parent-child relationship focuses so strongly on the attitudes and motivations of the parents, the expectations they hold for their children. The reader is probably asking, But what if the baby won't play? Are babies helpless? Don't they help shape the dialogue? Doesn't each baby have his or her own way of organizing experience? Will the baby's characteristics modify those of the parents and caregivers?

Thus far I have been stressing the role of the parents simply because, in the therapeutic context, it is possible to modify the interaction and thus have an effect upon the baby only through the caregiver, generally the mother, by modifying her fantasies, expectations, and anxieties. As soon as she starts talking about the baby, the mother uncovers her psychic state, offering us access to her inner world.

Babies do not let us into their private worlds so easily. Since babies have no words, they can express their feelings and wishes only through their bodies and through body language. This makes it difficult to get a clear picture of the intimate experience of babies.

And yet the baby is not a passive being. From the beginning, every child has an individual nature that will determine the attitudes of the parents and the nature of their mutual interactions.

Babies are active agents, and as we shall see, they have extraordinary power over their parents.

Heredity

It has never been incontrovertibly demonstrated that any given attitude or behavior pattern is hereditary. On the other hand, certain forms of depression, for instance, do seem to be transmitted by a genetic mechanism. Studies on the astonishing resemblance of the way identical (that is, monozygotic) twins behave have emphasized the role of heredity. But the similarities in behavior demonstrated by identical twins are due not just to the identity of their genes, but also to their shared environment and to the identifications that they presumably make with each other. More progress is needed in research on the genetic causes of behavior before any definitive statements can be made. All that is known for certain is that each baby is different, both on the psychic and on the behavioral levels.

Environmental (as opposed to hereditary) influences on a baby begin before birth, in the course of the nine months of pregnancy. It is becoming clearer and clearer that many factors influence the development of the fetus. The mother's body is the equivalent of an ecological niche for the fetus, and the special characteristics of that environment will influence the baby.

It is well known that the unborn child will react to certain things the mother does—her drinking, her smoking, the food she eats, the medications she takes, and so on. Poor nutrition will stunt the fetus's growth, and malnourished newborns are often irritable because their organic equilibrium has been interfered with.

Soon we shall probably be able to study the part played by the mother's emotional state during pregnancy. This will answer the questions of the many mothers who assure me that the anxiety or depression they experienced during pregnancy must have affected their children.

The Baby's Signature

Anyone who examines newborn babies cannot fail to be struck by their individuality. The idea that each baby is a person is unavoidable.

Let us take two examples. In the course of the standard examination of newborns, the baby is subjected to a certain number of frustrations: he is prevented from moving his legs, for example. Some babies start to wriggle and then cry, others manage to comfort themselves—by sucking a thumb. This ability to find a thumb and use it to get comfort is a remarkable resource that allows the child to escape from the constraints being imposed. It is not hard to see how important this self-protective ability will prove to be in the course of the child's development.

The other example centers on a feature that may be called "consolability." When a baby cries in distress, an adult cannot resist the desire to comfort him. Some babies calm down merely if someone talks to them. Others have to be picked up and held with their heads nestled in the crook of the adult's neck. In this position, a certain number of babies calm down, but others stiffen, unable to mold themselves to the shape of the adult body. Such babies are difficult to comfort. Different reactions of this kind have an enormous effect on parents or adult caregivers. When we succeed in quieting a child down, we have a feeling of competence. When the child persists in crying, we feel like failures. An inexperienced and insecure mother risks feeling rejected by a child who, by his or her reactions, does not offer her the chance to be a "good mother."

Each baby reacts to stimulation in a particular way.

When cold air is blown on her stomach, Baby A's heart rhythm goes up from 90 to 180 beats. Baby B will change only from 100 to 130. This shows that Baby A reacts with great intensity whereas Baby B is less easily excited. Differences in excitability will translate into behavior patterns. Baby A will have a very strong reaction to the attentions of those around, while Baby B will take everything much more calmly.

Each baby, from the very beginning, has a characteristic profile of sensitivity and activity. This individualism is like a signature that the mother—if she is taking notice—will learn to recognize, adapting her caregiving to the baby's capacity for receiving it.

This basic temperament is probably the result of the combined effects of heredity and intrauterine experience. It will determine behavior that, in its turn, will influence the parents and direct the course of the interactions.

Finding a Comfortable Fit

As we saw earlier, mother and baby together organize a form of exchange that is typical of them. Some of these dialogues are characterized by excitement, intensity, and activity. Others will be calm, placid, and silent. As these "styles" are shaped, babies contribute their own needs, and each one will have a specific tolerance threshold for stimuli. There are hypersensitive babies who startle at the slightest noise. Others, on the contrary, actively seek out stimulation.

This raises the question of attunement between the partners. Certain mothers have no problem with a first child who is placid but are then completely at a loss to deal with a second child who howls and shows what he wants in no uncertain terms. Such a mother will tend to interpret the second child's tears of hunger as voracious and excessively demanding.

Every mother-baby couple must therefore find some common ground on which the sensibilities of each are respected. Often it is the failure of reciprocal attunement that makes mothers anxious. They come to my consulting room with a sense of impotence.

Special Challenges

Let's first take two extreme examples to illustrate the baby's influence on the interaction.

Premature Babies   It is now possible to save premature babies weighing less than two pounds. Their lack of physical maturity makes the behavior of such babies difficult to interpret. They shift rapidly from sleep to waking, their cries are often high pitched, their movements jerky. It is hard to know what they need. Their appearance—worried, fragile, emaciated—is also upsetting. Parents are afraid of touching them and often get hyperactive, as if they wanted to compensate for the baby's lack of activity. When you watch a mother interacting with a premature baby, it is noticeable how anxious her behavior is. If you take the pulse of both partners, it turns out that the baby's pulse goes up during the exchanges, as if the maternal anxiety were contagious.

With the proper support and encouragement, a dialogue can begin. All that is necessary is that the mother base her behavior on the baby's own. When she comes down to the level of the infant's demands, the heartbeat of both drops because a better interactive harmony has been reestablished.

This example shows that the immaturity in the baby's conduct leads to an anomaly in the mother's, and at the same time provokes physiological changes, such as an accelerating pulse rate. This shows how powerful the baby's contribution is, causing simultaneously a disturbance in the mother's attitude as well as physical changes.

Blindness   When the baby has some kind of defect, communication can break down even more easily between mother and child. With a baby born blind, the normal program of interaction is completely upset. The mother cannot read the baby's mind from his or her expression and is therefore at a loss since the exchange of looks plays a crucial role in communication. In fact, following the birth, it is usually when the mother first meets the baby's eyes that the bonding process begins.

Blind children will not be able to smile when the mother's face comes close. They will not hold out their arms to be picked up, will show no interest in objects, and will react to a caregiver only through voice and touch. These limitations force mothers to adapt in an extraordinary way, and all too often we see confusion interfere in the mother-child exchanges.

Specialized intervention is very effective in these cases. The mother is shown, among other things, how babies communicate through touch. In fact, it is through a subtle use of their hands that blind babies show what they want and need. Some training is needed to understand these signs.

The Bonding Cycle

There has been considerable research on situations in which a baby comes into the world without the normal range of behaviors and abilities, as when he or she is premature or blind. Such research indicates that bonding between parents and child depends on certain programmed, innate activities that successfully ensure that the process of reciprocal commitment is engaged.

As we saw earlier, almost from birth the baby is intelligent enough to pick up those signs that mean "mother." The baby is attracted by the mother's face, smell, and voice. This attraction is strengthened by the pleasure the baby experiences from contact with the mother and comforts brought by her care and feeding.

But the adult is also attracted by the baby. It has been discovered that in higher animals the very shape of the baby automatically triggers protectiveness and affection in the parent. The shape of the baby's head in particular evokes this response. The large, round forehead occupying the upper half of the face and the chubby cheeks almost infallibly evoke tenderness in adults.

A baby's crying is also a powerful motivator. Few adults are indifferent to it. When the baby begins to smile, first, at around four weeks, in response to the voice and then, in the second month, to a face that comes close, the parents are sure that the baby loves them. Tears, smiles, eye contact, all act directly on the parents' affections, and bonding is ensured every time the baby acts in this way.

Parents place such value on these manifest "proofs" of the baby's attachment that they will do anything to make the exchanges continue. As soon as they notice that some shared experience gives pleasure, they will seek to repeat it. An intense dialogue is set up and then maintained by this mutual gratification.

The Power of Refusal

Just as parents feel gratified by a baby's obvious pleasure, so they will be adversely affected by a refusal.

One of the baby's most powerful acts is to say no:
no to food, no to exchange, no to affection. This
negativity can drive mothers to despair since they interpret it as rejection of what they have to offer.

The first time the baby takes the breast is a crucial
moment. As the baby nurses with more or less vigor,
the mother estimates his or her gastronomic enthusiasm
accordingly.

Yet many babies have trouble adapting to the
shape of the breast. At first, some are in no hurry to eat
and they fall asleep after taking a few sucks. It even
happens sometimes that newborn babies turn their
heads away after the first suck. What a blow to the
mother's self-esteem! She joyfully anticipates nursing her
child, whose first act is to turn away in refusal.

In fact, most often such initial problems arise because the baby is clumsy and the mother anxious and
uncertain of her new role. But very rapidly, if no one
intervenes, a vicious circle can be set up. The refusal
forces the mother to insist, and the more she insists the
more recalcitrant the baby gets. The situation soon gets
impossible—each feeding is a drawn-out contest, each
mealtime a fight.

A couple came to consult me about their baby, Alex, three months old. The parents were at the end of their tether. Alex refused to eat—meals lasted an hour and a half and amounted to an armed confrontation. As soon as Alex was laid down horizontally in his mother's arms and the bottle was produced, he acted in a characteristic fashion. He arched his back, with only his head and heels pressed against his mother's body. He howled, wriggled, and turned his head away to avoid the bottle. The mother stressed one thing in particular: the baby refused to look at her during these painful meals. The parents had tried every kind of maneuver. Alex got the better of them by refusing to cooperate.

It is impressive to see the impact the baby's strategy has on the parents. They feel completely impotent, unable to understand what is going on. Their life has been turned upside down by this feeding war that they feel they are losing.

Once Alex's brief life history had been taken, some glimmers of understanding became possible. His mother was eager to nurse him herself, but soon after his birth, she developed a cracked nipple, not an uncommon problem at the beginning of breast feeding. To prevent further damage, the nurses had supplied the mother with a nipple shield to be used during feeding. Alex got used to this and sucked quite satisfactorily.

After two weeks, the crack had healed and the mother tried to remove the nipple shield. This is when things started to go wrong. Alex demanded the nipple shield back. A few days later another change occurred. The mother's milk began to dry up and she quickly tried bottle feeding. From that day, Alex began his active resistance. It even became necessary to hospitalize him because he was losing weight.

When I asked to watch the baby being fed, I was struck by the way Alex anticipated what was happening. As soon as his mother laid him down in her arms, he stiffened, got excited, then turned his head away as the bottle came close. The direction of Alex's head seemed very significant to me: he turned his head away from the bottle and pressed it into his mother's breast!

The mother said to me, "He's looking for my arm!" I corrected her: "He's rooting for your breast. He doesn't want to forget it, and what he is refusing is the change." In fact, Alex had already had to put up with several changes: first the nipple shield, which he accepted, only to have it taken away, and finally the brusque change from breast to bottle. In twenty days of life he had already gone through three changes in routine that for him must have seemed like revolutions.

Thus Alex had become attached to the breast, and then to the nipple shield. When they were taken away, a habit was violated that was already charged with pleasure and that had offered him a sure source of comfort. That attachment and the memory of the pleasure that he had had at the breast, with the nipple shield, was already so well established *twenty days after birth* that a change in routine led Alex to revolt. By refusing to feed, Alex was demanding a return to a familiar status quo whose advantages he was unwilling to lose. When he turned his face away from the bottle to press it into his mother's breast, he was saying clearly and uncompromisingly that he wanted to return to the familiar pleasure of nursing. The memory of that first experience was already fixed firmly enough for him to refuse to give it up.

This child's behavior shows how strong attachments can be, how stubborn a baby's choice, how effectively the baby can put pressure on his family.

In this refusal to change and insistence on keeping a satisfying habit, there is surely the signature of a personality, the mark of a will. The parents were not slow to give their own meaning to Alex's behavior: "He has a will of iron. There's no way to make him give in." One cannot but acknowledge the powerful effect that this child's choice had on his parents. It is not hard to imagine how such a trial of strength could open up a lifelong confrontation between parents and child.

This example clearly shows the contribution the baby makes to starting and maintaining a specific form of interaction that will then develop according to the partners' ability to make compromises between them. For reasons arising out of this mother's history, she was unable to come up by herself with a satisfactory accommodation with her child. She had been unable to realize how attached Alex had become to the breast and that it was the change to bottle feeding, not her as his mother, that he was refusing. Once this problem had been explained, the conflict was defused. The baby gradually began to accept the bottle now that the situation was less charged. The situation of armed combat that had continued at mealtimes for more than two months was the result of a combination of factors in a strong-willed mother and child. He was not willing to give up the breast and she was unwilling to recognize how important it was to him.

No to the World

As soon as babies are born, they make choices. They can proclaim their interest in the people around them, their eagerness for food, their longing for exchanges. Such positive reactions generally lead parents to seek to be positive in their turn.

But babies can also make a statement by withdrawing: they may refuse the breast at the first attempt to nurse, may avoid eye contact, may refuse to react to any effort to engage their attention. Certain babies are called impassive: they show little or no emotion. Their facial expressions are so solemn that they make the people around them feel excluded or ignored. This refusal to engage can happen very early. It is the first no to social exchange.

There are also cases in which babies, from the second half of the first year, seem to lose interest in the world around them. They lie there calmly looking at the ceiling, refusing to react to their parents' attentions, neglecting the toys offered them. Their faces are expressionless. They seem to be living in another world.

This refusal to reach out and respond may result from the incoherence of the parents' behavior. The child withdraws as if he or she had given up trying to adapt to the parents' erratic signals.

More rarely, the baby may be incapable of dealing with the sensory demands and messages from the surrounding world. Such a baby will try to keep in balance by refusing to engage.

Refusal to engage is particularly acute in autistic children, and subtle strategies are needed to allow the child to reestablish contact.

Babies Build Their World

In all this we see that babies are able very early on to function on complex levels of organization. They show that they have memories, that they view situations as positive or negative, and interpret events and exchanges.

With behavior that says no, the baby is defining an

experience as unacceptable, and showing preference for another to which he or she has a prior attachment. When Alex refused the bottle, it was because he saw it as an enemy, as the thing that symbolized his loss of the experience of the breast that he had already idealized. Thus he gave the bottle a meaning and thereby showed he was already functioning on a specifically human level: he constructed a personal world, based on a network of meanings.

The psychoanalysis of adults who conjure up their childish thoughts allows us to have a better understanding of the powerful influence of desires, aversions, and fantasies in the construction of this personal world.

As we have seen, however, this network of meanings is the outcome of two simultaneous currents: the meaning that babies attribute to every experience results from their own intrinsic needs, as well as from constraints on the part of their parents. Experience takes on meaning through the combining of those two factors. One reason why it is so fascinating to study the way parents and child behave together is because these interactions provide vivid evidence of this meeting between the psyche of the child and that of the parents.

The Line of Defense

If, from the beginning, babies can say no, this is because they have the ability to perceive experiences as the source of pain and anguish. Their first line of defense against this danger is refusal. By refusing a situation they spare themselves anguish. At the same time, they will also seek to defend themselves by refusing the mental image of that situation. Resistance begins in this way: babies bury their experiences of anguish by repressing the thoughts associated with them, and thus contributing to the accumulation of experiences that have become unconscious.

This unconscious will make itself known in indirect ways that neither parents nor child are able to understand. When a child refuses to eat, for example, this may be because he or she is afraid of taking food. This act is unconsciously experienced as an attack on the mother who has withdrawn access to her breast. Mother and child will persist vainly in a contest of wills over the bottle, whereas the "real" problem is the child's demand for the breast and his mother's refusal to provide it. Eventually, the child will forget the demand; it will sink into the unconscious because the hate that accompanies it causes too much anguish.

Soon the only thing left on the surface will be a pattern of avoidance, expressed as a systematic refusal to cooperate. Such a refusal can overflow into other areas. The baby may become an obstinate soul who refuses any kind of commitment that he does not initiate himself.

Thus the baby's very first line of defense is to say no. This resistance can show itself in many ways—turning the head away, refusing to react, or even, sometimes, falling asleep when someone is demanding attention. What a powerful weapon against annoying or painful assaults!

A Script with Two Authors

In an earlier section I briefly mentioned the story of twins, one of which, the boy, worried his mother. She felt that he was not as advanced as his sister and not sturdy enough. He had had many infections, and above all, he was unable to defend himself when his sister got bossy.

The mother had deduced that he was more vulnerable than his sister and that he would never be able to defend himself in life. At ten months there was already a marked difference between the two twins. Whereas the little girl was gregarious, smiling, and active, the little boy was solemn, withdrawn, and quiet. When the mother called to her daughter, the little girl would smile and look at her, but the little boy did not react and kept looking at his shoes.

In a typical exchange between the two children, the boy might be playing with a rattle; his sister grabs it from him and he starts to cry. His mother takes him on her lap and consoles him while gently telling the girl not to be so rough. This exchange expresses the mother's central theme: the boy is weak; he risks suffering from his sister's aggressiveness.

The scenario is dictated both by the boy's style and by the mother's personal history. The boy is habitually slow and stolid in his reactions and less able to impose his will on others. Moreover, he is developing more slowly than his sister—she learned to sit up before he did. These characteristics weight the balance when he is compared to his sister. His personal style, which is probably congenital, is perceived by his mother as evidence of weakness. Another parent might see it differently, and appreciate his quiet calm.

But the mother's perception of these characteristics in her son is colored, as we saw, by her own history. She had had a twin brother whom she dominated by her intelligence and strong will. This child had died of an unexplained illness and his death had profoundly marked his twin sister. Not surprisingly, she had carried over her own experience as a twin, and her guilt, when dealing with her own twins. She is afraid that her history of sister-brother rivalry will repeat itself and that her son will suffer by it. In her family, the boys were always the weak ones, and naturally this image of fragility is carried over to the new generation.

Dance Partners

Like an intricate dance, the mother-baby interaction is the outcome of two people repeating certain

characteristic steps—like theme songs—with both partners moving separately while responding in unison to
the rhythm and the beat.

The music is written by the two partners according
to their individual preferences and talents. The child will
contribute according to the limits of his temperament,
his needs, his sensitivities. The mother has a bigger
repertoire available to her because of her longer life
experience, but she too will be subject to peremptory
desires and taboos that prejudice her attitudes toward
her child. Every encounter is an interaction between
these two fields of force.

But the dance of life is not just a duo. A child is
born of the joint desire of a mother and a father. Both
will bring their own dreams and expectations to the
parental role, and the choreography will become still
more complex.

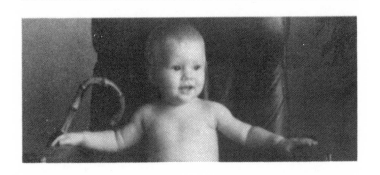

EIGHT

When the Plot Thickens

❦

*W*hen a baby arrives, a family of two becomes three. This implies a change in routine, sometimes a revolution.

The long-awaited baby makes a noisy entrance. His or her needs cannot be taken lightly. His imperious demands must be satisfied. When she cries, it's an order; when he howls, it's a threat.

A baby's needs cannot be deferred. They require the constant attention of an adult. Too bad if that adult has other jobs to do, or needs of his or her own, or is beset with worries. The baby demands obedience.

You might say that the relationship is perfectly asymmetrical. Babies are entirely taken up with their own needs, and adults must be entirely at their disposition. Parents often say, "That child is so selfish!" and many have trouble accepting the constant altruism that is forced upon them.

If, in addition, the baby is fussy or has physical

problems (such as premature babies have), he or she becomes virtually a monster, wearing the parents out, transforming a dream into a nightmare. Such a situation can create great stress between the husband and the wife.

Beware the Picture-Book Baby

The early mother-baby relationship has been described too often as a cloudless idyll. Circumstances such as a difficult labor, a premature delivery, or an excessively small apartment can sometimes turn the first encounter of mother and child into a nightmare. In some cases, parents may feel incompetent because they are unable to calm a baby who starts screaming. The mother may feel inadequate, her milk dries up, her patience is exhausted. Every mother will tell you that there was at least one moment when she wanted to throw the baby out the window. This, too, adds a weight of guilt to the relationship.

The parents become so exhausted and discouraged that the idyllic stereotype out of women's magazines is replaced by a bad dream. It is not surprising that many such parents are asking for professional help. Doctors who specialize in treating early childhood problems have to be ready to respond to these needs.

I think it would be useful to spread the idea that,

at the beginning, relations with a baby can be upsetting and full of disappointment. Parents have to realize that any painful disillusion they may feel is a result of the gap between the ideal baby they had imagined and the real baby they have. We also have to demystify the parent-baby relationship and explain that it can bring pain as well as pleasure. Babies can arouse the hatred of their parents, just as they can inspire parents' adoration.

On one level, it seems unthinkable that a baby could be hated: Isn't a baby the very symbol of innocence? Nonetheless, evil images that haunt the parents can be projected immediately upon the baby, who thereby becomes the epitome of all that is most hateful.

One mother came to consult me about her son Fabrice, seven years old, who had outbursts of aggression. When the mother narrated the story of life with Fabrice, this is what she told me about his birth: "He was three weeks late. He *would not* come. The first time I saw him he was all green and filthy. He was incredibly demanding, constantly wanting to be at the breast. We had to do what he wanted!" From the beginning, Fabrice had been seen as an evil person, his needs tyrannical, his appearance foul, and his nature greedy.

Relations between these two went from bad to worse. This particular mother in fact felt the need to keep everything in her world under close control. She could not put up with the child having *his* way. What was more, she was intensely house-proud and tidy and therefore loathed any kind of dirt or mess. It turned out that she would have preferred a daughter and thought all men were "pigs."

A projection as strong and unmitigated as this is hard to change. It tends to be a self-fulfilling prophecy, as the child is seen as irredeemably bad.

While this case is extreme, we have to realize that a certain amount of hostility against the baby is naturally present in all of us, in all parents. We are all subject to a certain ambivalence because hostility coexists with love.

The black side of this ambivalence may appear as early as the third trimester of the pregnancy. Dreams appear in which the fetus is deformed or disfigured. Fears that the baby will be abnormal become insistent. "And what if the baby is a monster, not an angel?" the parents seem to say.

It is hard to imagine that behind these fears lurks a certain hostility toward the expected baby. Nonetheless, psychoanalysis reveals that a woman, even if she has intensely desired her pregnancy, can harbor hatred for the fruit of her own womb. Fathers too can experience this hatred, although usually it remains unconscious.

If the fetus is unconsciously confused with one of the parent's little brothers, that parent will carry over onto the unborn child all the jealousy and hate felt in early childhood.

If the mother's pregnancy has caused a child to feel an intense rage that is usually forgotten afterwards, this anger will be reactivated when the child becomes a parent.

Such negative feelings will be all the more present if, at birth, the baby is difficult, disappointing, or resented as a tyrant.

The Baby Therapist

The task before the parents is thus shadowed by the influence of this unseen hatred that is so scandalous they cannot even acknowledge it. So the hate is expressed indirectly, through anxieties (above all the fear that the baby may die, that he will smother, or drown in his bath) or through a feeling of paralysis and ineptitude (the fear of not having enough milk, of being unable to deal with the baby's crying, and so on).

The best therapy for these feelings is the behavior of the baby himself. When the mother sees that the baby takes easily to the breast, that he is happy with the care she gives him, the dark side of ambivalence and its attendant fears will fade. Then, when the mother sees that the baby is becoming attached to her, smiles at her, asks for her, she will discover with relief that her most terrifying thoughts have had no effect on the child. When the mother succeeds in translating the baby's attachment into a sign of love, she can effectively neutralize her fears of harming him.

Sometimes, this is not enough. Parents may need an understanding professional to hear their distress and to allow them to confess their ambivalence. Then, little by little, negative feelings can be identified and accepted.

Jealous of the Baby

When a twosome becomes a threesome, there's a good chance that one of the three feels left out. Usually it's the father. Few of us realize how much men envy women's ability to have children. In certain traditional cultures, fathers undergo a kind of simulated pregnancy called the couvade. They take to their beds, groan in pain, and go through a kind of childbirth. What male power could possibly equal the creativity of pregnancy? What human competence could possibly be on the level of breast feeding? And even if many new fathers today show a talent for parenting that makes them as competent as their wives, it is rare to find a masculine equivalent of the visceral attachment that mothers have for their babies.

Much has been made in the past about the maternal instinct, nothing about paternal instinct. It is as if popular wisdom had decided once and for all that "maternal" caretaking is done more naturally by women than men.

In a unique and almost obsessed manner, the mother of the newborn baby becomes totally absorbed in her child. D. W. Winnicott calls this "primary maternal preoccupation." Just as we say that love is a madness that takes a person by storm, so new mothers experience a kind of madness. The baby becomes absolute master, and virtually all the mother's other interests are banished.

For the husband, this intimate union of mother and child is felt as an exclusion. He may react in different ways—go off, take a mistress, get drunk or depressed. Often he will have psychosomatic symptoms.

His relationship with the child will be colored by a jealousy that often takes the form of disinterest. He may criticize the baby, claim the baby is too willful, too bossy, needs to be trained, shown who's in charge. In his relationship with his wife, the father's feelings can take the form of resentment, lack of affection, even a total lack of sexual interest.

Mrs. Evans consulted me because her son Victor, two and a half, was being rough and disobedient. He refused to eat and this upset his mother so much that she was afraid she might beat him: "He's the only one that can really get to me."

Earlier in her life, Mrs. Evans had given up hope of getting any support from her own family and had therefore looked to find herself an adoptive family in the company where she was working. When she did not get the company promotion she thought was her due, she went into a depression and felt deeply resentful toward her bosses who had so disappointed her. It was at the beginning of that depression that she had conceived Victor, believing that the child would be her "salvation."

Unfortunately she did not tell her lover that she was planning to get pregnant, and he reacted very negatively when she told him a baby was on the way. "What a drag . . . now we'll have to get married!" From the time of the birth, the father kept his distance from mother and child, spending all his time reading on the balcony or watching television.

Mrs. Evans became even more depressed when she admitted to herself, "I should never have had a child with him." Husband and wife entered a phase of psychological separation that made the mother feel she had failed to create a family. This was the third time that, in her own view, she had failed to find a family to which she could belong. Her pregnancy had been motivated by the desire to re-create not only her own original family but also the borrowed family she believed she had found at work. The breakup with her lover, on both the emotional and sexual levels, had been hastened by her secret decision to have a child. Faced with the accomplished fact of the pregnancy, her lover felt she had deceived him. He also, for reasons relating to his personal history, was unable to accept the presence of a third person. Thus the presenting symptom—Victor's aggressiveness—came straight out of the atmosphere of conflict between husband and wife.

In a case like this, one can see how one partner's desire for a child can conflict with the needs of the other. The coming of the real child can cause bitter conflict and thus tear a couple apart.

When reactions of this kind are deep and lasting, their effects can be seen on the mother-baby relationship. The mother may feel lonely and left to cope by herself with the baby's demands or, on the other hand, she may seek some emotional compensation from the baby, who becomes a substitute lover. Such a combination—exclusion of the father and fusing of the bonds between mother and child—entails grave risks for the child's development.

The Baby and Sexuality

In almost all my consultations with mothers about the difficulties they are having with their child, I uncover a problem of sexual difficulties between husband and wife and even a threat of the couple breaking up.

For a woman, a lessening in libido often results from a fear of pain, whether it be the pain associated with an episiotomy scar (incision left by the obstetrician) or, simply, the memory of labor and childbirth. Often there is a fear of sexual relations that are imagined as violent.

In the case of Sebastian—which I discussed earlier in Chapter 5—the mother consciously avoided sexual relations with her husband. She was afraid of them just as she was afraid of her son's "roughness," just as she had always been afraid of attacks on her body's integrity.

This fear was a clear-cut symptom. This young woman experienced extreme anxiety when her husband made advances to her. It was obvious that in her imagination the way that her baby had torn her body (he had occasioned a cesarean section and had caused her pain while nursing) amounted to a kind of rape. She saw sexual relations in the same way. As it turned out, as soon as her anxiety about the baby's "roughness" waned, she was able to resume a normal sex life.

For men, libido may decline because of the resentment caused by the baby taking over the mother's body. In both sexes, the central conflict is connected to a reemergence of the whole oedipal issue for the parents. The baby's coming recreates a triangular situation resembling the one the parents had experienced with their own parents during childhood. Feelings of rivalry, exclusion, hatred, and guilt are once again at work, creating a new edition of the ancient conflict. The most common form this takes is the creation of a mother-baby complicity that excludes the father. Old resentments reemerge. The mother feels that her husband is repeating the indifference of her father. The husband, on the other hand, feels deprived of his wife's love, just as once his father had forbidden him possession of his mother. As the hostility builds, sexual desire weakens, and husband and wife drift apart.

When a Baby Destroys the Triangle

As we have just seen, in many situations the baby's arrival, far from being a couple's greatest joint achievement, serves to break husband and wife apart. But there are also cases when the baby's conception will threaten the relationship between the parent (father or mother) and his or her own parents.

Such situations demonstrate how much the wish for a child results from the oedipal relationship each parent has to his or her own parents. The child's coming can be felt as a wound inflicted upon the grandparents, or as the equivalent of a victorious rivalry (with parents supplanting their own parents by their creativity), or it may signal the irrevocable cutting of the umbilical cord still linking parents to their parents.

Prospective grandparents often react in the most amazing way to news that their children are expecting. One remark often heard from the lips of prospective grandmothers when speaking to their daughters is "Now you will know what I went through when I had you!" It's as if she is able to bear her daughter's access to motherhood only if she can hand on the torch of maternal suffering and the image of the mater dolorosa.

Let me describe one case in which the oedipal drama was played out with fatal exactness.

Mrs. Gross was sent to me by her pediatrician because Samuel, aged nine months, had extreme difficulty getting to sleep. Typically, Samuel would scream, his mother would wake up and go to him, rock him, and finally, weary of the struggle, take him into bed with her. The mother was obviously exhausted.

In my office, I was immediately struck by the singular character of the interaction that took place before my eyes. Whereas most mothers would keep a child of this age on their lap—at least at the beginning of the session—Mrs. Gross immediately places Samuel on the floor. He then throws up, she cleans him up, and puts him right back on the floor.

She keeps the baby at a distance in this way throughout most of the session. I cannot understand why, as Mrs. Gross appears to be a loving person. She is neither depressed nor, I am sure, does she lack interest in her child.

When finally she does take him on her lap, once again the two interact in a very unusual way. She holds him standing up on her knee, with his face turned away from her. Exchanges between the two are short, awkward, lacking in the harmony characteristic of relaxed interactions, and lacking, above all, in bodily contact. Several times, Samuel turns his head toward his mother, trying to touch her with his mouth. Each time, the mother maintains the distance between them.

The impression I get from this observation is that there is some barrier to close contact, as if the mother wants to avoid her son's advances. I feel the child's frustration as he fails to establish a body dialogue with her. The two never come together.

There is a striking agreement between what I see and what the mother tells me. She explains the essentials of her educational philosophy. She is trying to leave her son alone as much as possible and avoids picking him up because she doesn't want him to "become too attached to her." "It would be bad for him to be clinging to my skirts all the time."

What can be the origin of such ideas? These principles seem to determine the distance she maintains in her interactions with Samuel. What makes her believe bodily contact is so harmful?

An Ominous Beginning

During the days following her daughter's announcement that a baby was on the way, Mrs. Gross's mother behaved in a completely unexpected way. She wrote to her daughter explaining that she was going to commit suicide because of some great sin she had on her conscience. Mrs. Gross rushed over to her mother's house and was told that her mother had a lover. This piece of news spreads, the father hears of it, husband and wife have a major crisis, and the mother, unable to bear the results of her own confession, has to get psychiatric help.

Mrs. Gross, scared out of her wits by this whole development, is convinced that it is the announcement of her pregnancy that has destroyed the balance of her parents' marriage. Over the next months she will be haunted with the fear that her mother will take her own life.

In the seventh month of Mrs. Gross's pregnancy, her mother decides to leave her husband, and to convey this news, she again chooses to write a letter. Mrs. Gross intercepts the letter because she is convinced that her father would not be able to bear the shock of the news and would commit suicide.

All of this goes on in an atmosphere of acute anxiety and tension. Mrs. Gross is far more caught up in her parents' problems than with her own pregnancy. The next ultrasound, also in the seventh month, reveals that the pregnancy is not going well. The fetus has stopped growing, apparently just at the time when the grandparents have finally separated. The gynecologist explains to Mrs. Gross that her nervous condition is probably not unrelated to the baby's problem. Shortly afterwards, the doctors perform a cesarean to relieve fetal distress, and the baby just barely pulls through. At the time of the birth, no one shows Mrs. Gross the baby and she therefore concludes that he is dead.

When there is a failure of growth, a child's whole organism may suffer. When Samuel is six months old, it is noted that he is slow to sit up on his own and that his musculature is weak. These neurological signs are very probably due to the disturbance in his development in utero and to the distress he suffered there. His mother's fear that he would die at birth was thus far from unfounded.

The circle was complete. For Mrs. Gross, the death of her parents' marriage *had to* coincide with the death of her baby. It was the law of retaliation. Convinced that she was responsible for producing a stream of disasters through her announcement that she was pregnant, she was expecting her child to die because he had killed his grandparents' marriage.

Child of Incest

But why did Mrs. Gross have to attribute such evil power to her pregnancy? How could a baby destroy his grandparents' marriage?

The triangle binding Mrs. Gross to her parents was to be demolished by the imposition of another triangle: the triangle of incest. Here a distinction must be made between real incest—sexual relations between parent and child—and fantasized incest that occurs only in the imaginations of those involved.

Yet this imaginary form may have very far-reaching effects, particularly if it fits into a certain family reality. In Mrs. Gross's family, this reality took the following form.

When my second scheduled visit with Mrs. Gross came around, I was greeted in the waiting room by an alert fifty-year-old man in sports gear, who declares, "I am the father."

I am at a loss for words. I am amazed that Samuel's father would be this old. However, keeping my thoughts to myself as a psychiatrist should, I greet him without further remarks, and Mrs. Gross follows me into my office, leaving the "father" behind.

She immediately explains, with a nervous laugh, that the gentleman is her own father. He devotes a great deal of time to her and has offered to drive her over. The discussion turns to her own relations with her parents. Her mother has recently complained that she is always wrapped up in her father and spends no time with her. The grandmother explains that if she doesn't come to see her daughter often (in fact, the two have been estranged since the pregnancy) it is because she feels *unwelcome.*

Mrs. Gross's mother feels left out in the father-mother-daughter triangle. In fact she has always been jealous of the very close relation of father and daughter. Mrs. Gross admits that her father has been even more attached to her since the separation. During the days after Samuel's birth, he came to the maternity hospital every day, and Mrs. Gross had even felt embarrassed when her mother dropped in unexpectedly one day and found her father sitting on her bed.

One part of the script emerged quite clearly here: the rapprochement between father and daughter coincides with the separation of the parents and with Samuel's arrival on the scene. That ambiguous remark made by the (grand)father—"I am the father"—has to be interpreted as an incest fantasy. He sees himself as Samuel's father, and his daughter goes along with the script. This is shown by the fact that, on the one hand, Mrs. Gross is convinced that her parents split up when she announced she was pregnant and, on the other hand, that she has so far said nothing at all to me about her husband, Samuel's biological father.

The initial oedipal triangle of mother-father-daughter has been destroyed by the coming of a new triangle, the one that makes Samuel the imaginary fruit of incest between father and daughter.

As Mrs. Gross becomes conscious of this incestuous switch, she recalls always having been afraid that her
father might make an advance toward her. She remembers having had to share a bed with her father when she
was a child and being terrified that he would touch her.

When Mrs. Gross brings up her fear of being
touched by her father, I glimpse a relationship between
this fear of incest and her relationship with Samuel. I
say to her, "You are as afraid of touching Samuel now
as you were once afraid of physical contact with your
father." She then confirms this interpretation by saying
that she had indeed developed a particular strategy for
bringing up her baby because she was so sensitive to
the reproaches that her family had made to her. As
soon as Samuel was born, she had been warned not to
spoil her son and not to give in to him when he wanted
to be picked up. *Her mother* in particular had criticized
her for showing the baby too much physical affection.

Obviously the reason why she had taken these
criticisms so much to heart was that she was afraid that
her tenderness would be seen as incestuous. She was
afraid of reproducing with Samuel that forbidden loving
relationship binding a parent and a child of the opposite
sex.

Unconsciously, Samuel was the fruit of incest. This
relationship had to be declared taboo, and I had been
able to see that taboo situation acted out in the
mother-child encounters. Mrs. Gross systematically

avoided responding to Samuel's demands, as if they were *sexual advances.*

She felt it necessary to restrain her affectionate impulses, keep a distance between them, and avoid any contact that could be misinterpreted. How strange that she should direct her actions to the wrong person. She thought she was doing the right thing in imposing detachment on Samuel; by frustrating her son she was, in her imagination, putting a barrier up against her father's advances.

Oedipal Conflicts across the Generations

It is generally believed that the Oedipus complex is a structure that transcends experience, just like an innate predisposition. By this theory the baby would from the outset tend to resent the intrusion of a third party, desire the parent of the opposite sex, and seek to eliminate the parent of the same sex.

In practice, however, it is often possible to see how parents "act out" the oedipal conflict, forcing the baby to align himself according to the parents' own Oedipus complex. Thus it could be argued that the child's Oedipus complex is constructed to mirror his parents'. To the child's Oedipus corresponds a parental "counter-Oedipus."

We can see how this is worked out in the case of

Mrs. Gross's family. In the course of the therapy, an unexpected leap into the past occurred when it became apparent that the visible, even transparent, history of Mrs. Gross's incestuous tendencies was rooted in events one generation back, that is, in the childhood of her own mother.

Following the session in which we had brought to the surface her fear of getting close to Samuel and the way in which that fear was based on the fear of incest, Mrs. Gross had a conversation with her maternal grandmother. This lady revealed the following secret: Mrs. Gross's mother had been the victim of sexual assault at the age of four. Since that time she had always feared men and suspected that her husband—in his turn—was taking advantage of their daughter while she was a child.

When Mrs. Gross had her baby, it was her mother who "forbade" her once again to have any close physical contact, and this taboo was understood as a warning about the temptation of incest. After this taboo, Mrs. Gross determined to keep a vigilant distance from Samuel. By doing so she in her turn showed the distrust that her mother had conceived for men.

Once more the wrong person was being addressed. Mrs. Gross was treating Samuel as a partner in a sexual assault that had occurred two generations earlier. Here we see how a grandmother's trauma may dictate the sexual destiny of her grandson. One generation flows into the next. No sooner was Samuel born than he was imprisoned within a script for a sexual drama that had been played out fifty years earlier! At the age of a few months he has already been cast in the role of sexual pervert, and there is the risk that his fate will be influenced by this casting. If his mother had not managed to become aware of the identity that she was pinning on her child, she would have been forced to struggle constantly against the potential symptoms of perversity. In this way she would be keeping her son at a distance and would risk stifling every sexual impulse in him.

Given this scenario, how could Samuel have ever achieved a sexual identity untainted by clandestinity and perversion?

Yet Another Surprise

This story already seems complicated enough and we might hope to have gotten to the end of the chain of cause and effect. Because unconsciously she felt guilty of an incestuous attachment to her father, Mrs. Gross had imagined that it was her announcement that she was pregnant that had led to her parents splitting up. The incest issue, carried over onto Samuel, lay at the

root of her avoidance of contact. Now that this whole
scenario was out in the open, a richer interaction
between mother and son could be anticipated.

But getting to the heart of this drama depended
on our returning to the beginning of the catastrophic
chain of events that had brought Mrs. Gross to my office. Why had this woman been so convinced that she
had destroyed her parents' marriage? And why had her
mother reacted so violently to the announcement of her
pregnancy?

The reader may recall that Mrs. Gross's mother
had written a letter threatening suicide and accusing
herself of an unforgivable sin—taking a lover.

Imagine my amazement when I learned from Mrs.
Gross that this lover had been an intimate friend of her
own, a young ski instructor whom she had met at ski
competitions. A friendship had grown between the two
of them; so she was dumbfounded to find that her
mother had fallen in love with this man so much her
junior and who, moreover, had been in love with Mrs.
Gross herself.

She had been all the more astonished since her
mother was such an outspoken moralist and a stern
opponent of divorce. In fact, it was *the mother* who,
by intervening in her daughter's relationship, had
caused her to break up with her ski-instructor friend.
It now appeared that the whole situation had been set
in motion by *the mother's* jealousy of her daughter.

This mother, who had criticized so severely first the relationship of her daughter to her husband and then her daughter's relation to her child, had acted out of jealousy of her daughter, even to the point of stealing her lover away from her.

Rather than theorize that the mother's Oedipus complex is the root of the matter, and the daughter's is simply an offshoot, it may be preferable to think of actions fitting a pattern. Undoubtedly mother and daughter share a problem with jealousy, which leads each to intrude upon the intimate relationships of the other. These resonance effects lead one generation to mimic the other. Patterns of behavior are passed on, dramas unfold, and the same scenarios are repeated by parent and child.

The members of all families follow in each other's footsteps in this way. This is how a continuity of generations is assured and individual experience is situated within the family mythology. An individual cannot invent a personal history from scratch but must build on the lives of those who went before. But, sometimes, the transmission of family history is so knotted and narrowed that the range of possible fates is small. The baby at the end of the chain becomes the prisoner of prehistory.

Samuel was a prisoner in this way. He had been locked in the identity of a sexual pervert, and his mother felt herself directed to exert a corrective discipline. Her duty was to forbid her son to commit incest, and in so doing, she was depriving him of the pleasures of intimacy.

Loosening the Grip of the Past

Mrs. Gross was extremely relieved when she was able to talk to me about her fear of incest and her rivalry with her mother. She began to have many dreams in which she saw herself alone with Samuel, without her husband. This dream caused her great distress and she began to discuss her relationship with her husband, who up to this point had been excluded from our sessions. In fact, sexual relations between the spouses had ceased *since Mrs. Gross had been pregnant.*

Here we find another couple that has split up since baby came into the world: further proof that a birth is not always good news. On every level in this family, the child's conception had led to disruption, as if the desire for a child was incestuously motivated and hence needed to be punished.

Little by little, the triangles formed once again in their original configuration. Mrs. Gross reached out to her mother more successfully, and there were fewer wrangles between her parents. As for Samuel's difficulty with sleeping, which had brought this family to consult me in the first place, this disappeared once the mother realized that at night, under the cloak of darkness, she had been giving her son the intimate contact she refused him during the day. She was spending a long time hugging Samuel to her in bed, allowing herself to touch him in ways she was afraid to do during the day, for fear of the criticisms of her family.

When Mrs. Gross felt able to touch Samuel during the day, and when she and her husband had established a better relationship, there was no longer any reason for the hidden exchanges at night, and Samuel was able to sleep. He was now no longer viewed as a sexual pervert in need of correction.

The Father's Contribution

In this entire story the father seems barely a shadow. Several sessions were needed before Mrs. Gross was able to realize how her husband had been excluded, whether by her fault or his. It is quite common to find the father excluded in this way in consultations that concern problems with babies. As we have seen, the mother can become obsessed with the baby, caught up in the promise of an idyllic relationship for two. The baby takes over her life and she increasingly expects the baby to provide her with everything she ever wanted.

The husband, in turn, often contributes to his own exclusion. He turns away from the family circle, feeling he has no part to play there.

One of the most important ways of assisting a young family is probably to shore up the basic triangle of father-mother-child. However, the therapies I have been discussing usually concentrate on the mother and the child. Doesn't this reinforce the exclusion of the father? Shouldn't the father be brought into the sessions immediately? It might seem that infant psychiatry tends to privilege the mother's role to the point at which the mother becomes all-powerful in her relationship with the child, and solely responsible for the child's problems.

In practice, when conducting mother-baby therapy, we observe that even if the father is not physically present, he always appears at a crucial moment in the conversations.

This moment occurs precisely when the parents' relations with their own parents is brought to light and when the playing out of the old script is unmasked. This is because the mother cannot successfully exorcise her own ghosts until she finds a place for her child's father in the present. In other words, when she comes to a conscious realization of her oedipal feelings toward her parents, she at the same time "discovers" the real part played by the child's father. This was very clear in the case I have been discussing. When Mrs. Gross was able to freely express physical affection for Samuel, after having exorcised her rivalry with her mother and her fear of incest with her father—at this very point—her husband suddenly appeared on stage.

When I am successful in my therapy, there is always a moment when the mother's parents are put back in their rightful places and when the mother can recognize the role of her child's father. Thus, in my practice, the father's role is carried by the mother, and our work together in therapy must lead to the father being set back in his rightful place, first of all in her own internal world. A man can become a father only if his wife confers that status upon him.

NINE

The Second Birth

☙

As we have seen, the arrival
of a child can be based on a misunderstanding. In all
the cases I have been discussing, the babies were mistaken for someone else. They served as a screen on
which were projected images of actors who had once
played a part in the lives of their parents. These babies—who carry the promise of future achievements—
are, in a certain sense, frozen into repeating ancient
scenarios. Because of this, they are not perceived as new
beings, with their own characteristics. Often a whole
process of exorcism is necessary before the ghosts leave
the stage and the parents are able to discover their
baby. In successful therapy this process takes place and
the baby is born a second time.

Discovering Marie

In the beginning of this book, we witnessed the misunderstanding that thrust Marie into an ancient quarrel

between her grandmother and her mother. Through Marie, Mrs. Martin was reproaching her mother for lack of affection and mourning her separation. Evelyn Martin had singled out the wrong person, to such an extent that she was unable to see how much her daughter really needed her.

Soon after therapy began, the long-remembered slap was put back in the context of the old story. Evelyn was able to talk about her immense nostalgia for her mother, and at once, she no longer saw Marie as a threat of violence. But Evelyn had yet to discover that Marie could love her.

Protective Distance

During one session, Marie played at her mother's feet. Evelyn sat a few inches away from the child. The baby crept nearer and finally grabbed hold of the tip of her mother's shoe. Evelyn notices this, pulls her chair away, and reestablishes the distance. I point out to her that she has pulled back and note a coincidence: Evelyn has just been talking about the suffering she feels because her mother is so distant (both geographically and emotionally). Why is it that she is setting a distance between herself and Marie at the very moment when she is suffering from the separation from her own mother?

Evelyn explains then that Marie needs to learn to manage for herself or otherwise she will be miserable when she has to go to school.

I suggest to her that she appears to impose this distance as if she were afraid that Marie might cling to her. I add that if she is bringing Marie up to be able to do without any attachments, it's as if she were immunizing the child against a desperate attachment to her mother. Evelyn responds at once, "You're right—if I am like my mother, I pity her!"

By maintaining distance in her relationship with Marie, Evelyn thinks she can prepare her daughter for the disappointments involved in any attachment. She is afraid of being like her mother, afraid that Marie will have to suffer the same unresolvable nostalgia that haunts her own life.

A mother who immunizes her child against herself is surely inflicting the bitterest of punishments upon herself. Hence we are now better able to understand why Evelyn had complained about Marie's lack of affection toward her. Yet she herself had brought this disaffection about.

This was the turning point in the therapy. From this point on, Evelyn was able to discover her daughter. At the next session she reported that Marie was calmer and—above all—much more affectionate in her behavior. Mrs. Martin commented, "I don't know whether she has changed or whether I simply see her differently."

Evelyn's vision of her daughter has changed. Now she sees her with different eyes, or rather she recognizes the child's own face, without the face of her mother superimposed upon it.

"Though people do tell me," she says, "that Marie's whole expression has changed."

An extraordinary power inhabits these images that we carry within us and project, as though on a screen, on the faces of those around us.

Evelyn's new perspective brought about many changes, as though by conjuring up the love Evelyn had for her own mother we had shown her relationship to Marie in a wholly new light. First of all, Marie may now touch her mother's face without making her wince. Furthermore, Marie has begun to rush into her mother's arms each time they are reunited.

Marie has become much more lively. She smiles and approaches people in the most endearing way. Every time Marie smiles at her, I see Evelyn respond tenderly whereas earlier the exchanges between them had been rather sad and dispirited.

"She has become so easy to live with," Evelyn will say of her daughter. I am struck by this expression: a few sessions before Evelyn had said of her own mother, "There was no living with her." Life has returned: there has been a second birth.

Reparation

In my practice, the turning point usually occurs when the child is discovered and the ghostly images from the past are banished. When this happens, there is great relief: anxieties are under control. Suddenly new feelings are possible. The demands and the reproaches have been put back in place in the mother's former life, and once the child has been absolved of them they no longer stand in the way. The baby can be seen as a new being with whom there is no quarrel. A détente is declared, and love can be exchanged once more. The child, who had been a source of anguish, finds his or her place as a partner in pleasure.

Hope is also reborn as expectations concerning the child's future are purged of negative predictions.

The family calms down. A new order prevails. The oedipal triangles return to their original form. Intergenerational conflicts take on another dimension as the two married partners take on the status of parents. These stages of reorganization go along with visible changes in behavior. Contact replaces distance; family members engage with, instead of avoid, each other.

The baby's behavior, which had looked so alarming, now seems quite innocuous, and exchanges are now overtly reciprocal. At the heart of all this transformation is a change in the parents' image of the child.

It's as if a broken picture had been mended. Then the parent feels competent once more. Evelyn Martin was particularly gratified to note that she was now able to make Marie smile; from now on she was sure that she could make Marie happy.

Russian Dolls

As parents rediscover their child, they also rediscover their own parents. As the image of the child is repaired, so also is the image of the grandparents.

During one of our last sessions, I witnessed a very touching interaction. Evelyn had Marie curled up in her arms. Marie was holding a stuffed lamb in her own arms and was hugging the toy tenderly. Evelyn interrupted what she was telling me to comment, "That's the very first time Marie has done that," as if she was discovering her daughter's readiness to show affection and even mother her lamb. I said to Mrs. Martin that she and her daughter were like the Russians dolls that fit inside one another. The mother hugs her daughter, who in turn hugs her stuffed animal. This is how Marie would discover her identity as a future mother, I suggested.

Evelyn continued the same idea. She hated it when people criticized her mother without having any appreciation of her mother's special qualities. Evelyn remembered the great sacrifices her mother had made to bring her up despite her mother's difficult situation as an immigrant.

She went on: "I understand now: you can only be with your child the way your mother was with you!" The circle was complete. The set of Russian dolls I was watching had opened up to reveal one more inside. Marie was able to hug her toy lamb only because she had been hugged by her mother. And that scene was possible only because Evelyn had managed to create in her mind the image of her own mother holding Evelyn in her arms.

Reparation had occurred on several levels. By repairing the image of her mother—whom on this day she was portraying in a very new light—Evelyn had been able to see her daughter's love, thereby making Marie a potential mother. It's not only scenarios of conflict and deception that are transmitted from generation to generation. The capacity for love also flows from one level to another. The work of therapy consists in wakening the capacity to perceive these dormant links of affection.

A Few Months Later

When Marie was two, Mrs. Martin called to tell me that her daughter was having trouble sleeping. She would refuse to go to bed and cling to her mother, forcing her at times to spend the night on the couch in the living room.

When I asked for some details about what happened in the evenings, a typical scene emerged. Evelyn would tell her daughter that it was bedtime, saying, "Say goodnight to Daddy." Marie would refuse and have to be forced to give her father a kiss. This would lead to a quarrel in which the child would hit her father. The mother was forced to intervene and put her to bed in an extremely tense atmosphere.

Recently Mr. Martin had had to work late, and when he was not at home Marie went off to bed without any problems. Marie seemed to be experiencing her father as the person who signaled separation between mother and daughter and the beginning of a night of loneliness. He was the intruder in the family triangle, and when Marie hit him she was expressing resentment and jealousy.

Evelyn confirms my impressions: "Yesterday evening Marie cried for a long time when she saw me give my husband a little kiss."

Marie is clearly suffering from the effect of her oedipal rivalry. She wants to keep her mother to herself and exclude her father. Marie is showing her jealousy through her difficulties in sleeping. She is too disturbed to be able to fall asleep when she knows her parents are busy "giving each other a little kiss."

Shared Jealousy

As I explained earlier, the oedipal jealousy of children is strengthened by that of their parents. Therefore I asked Marie's father to come in so that I could evaluate his part in this scene of nocturnal exclusion.

During several conversations we held in the presence of his wife and child, Mr. Martin explained how mortified he felt that his daughter showed him so little affection. He complained that when he arrived home and tried to embrace his wife, Marie would get so upset that she was a real "circuit breaker." He felt he was out of the "network," pushed aside, neglected. (The father's electrical expressions were related to his work as a streetcar driver.) All this made him feel so abandoned that he wept. He then agreed that some fathers might feel jealous and explained that in his childhood he had felt torn away from his mother by his father's violent scenes. Thus Mr. Martin had also been excluded from the first triangle he had known, and his conflict with Marie was due to the reemergence of his feeling of being, once again, odd man out.

Instead of offering to become an alternative to her mother for Marie, he had resented Marie as a hated rival. Hence the quarrels between father and daughter. Again, one thing fits inside another. Marie's insomnia is the equivalent of a jealous tantrum that fits a similar feeling in her father, who had also suffered from being excluded as a child.

Once the pieces of this puzzle had been put together, the triangle of mother-father-Marie could be reestablished. At the same time, Evelyn changed her way of putting Marie to bed, and the trouble with sleeping disappeared rapidly.

The reader may remember that at the time of the first consultation—when Marie was thirteen months old—her mother had complained, among other things, that Marie was lacking in affection. She explained that she herself was reluctant to hold the baby in her arms because her family had reproached her for spoiling the child. Now that we are aware of the father's psychological situation, we can judge that Evelyn was forbidding herself close contact with Marie also because she did not want to arouse her husband's jealousy. She knew how much he suffered from feeling excluded.

This case shows clearly that the child is deeply affected by the histories of both parents. The mother-child relationship is shaped around the father's attitude. The development of the mother-child bond depends on that of the mother-father bond.

Causes of the Child's Problems

I have explored the story of Marie in such detail because I wanted to illustrate the infinite complexity of the forces that decide the fate of a child.

We have seen how an old relationship rooted in the generation preceding the newborn baby is projected onto the mother-child relationship. The exchanges of violence and love between two generations have a similar form.

However, the interaction between father and daughter also fit directly into his own life story. Furthermore, for a problem to arise—that is, psychic suffering that provokes certain symptoms—children have to develop their own way of reacting to pressure upon them. Every child interprets the scripts dictated by the projections and interactions with parents according to his or her own personality. The child brings his own desires and fantasies to bear as well as a predisposition either to create conflict or to find harmonious solutions.

In the stories I have told I have laid particular stress on the effect of the encounter between the parents and the child, and I have emphasized the scenarios induced by the parents. It is in this scenario as it is acted out in the interaction between the two protagonists that mother-baby psychotherapy is effective.

In my practice, I especially emphasize parental projections as "causes" of infantile problems. But as we have seen, it is crucial not to stop at the first layer of causation. Again and again we have come to the realization that one cause may hide another.

Behind the mother there is the grandmother, and behind her a whole line of ancestors. The father-mother-baby triangle is organized in terms of the original triangles of both mother and father.

This chain of causation is itself affected by other influences. There is the weight of the culture that molds child-rearing philosophies and practice; there is the force of specific events as well as a spirit of the times that subtly influence our thoughts and our options. It is never possible to isolate one single cause.

The Evolving Adult

Throughout the growth of a human being, another set of influences will play a fundamental role: the events that a child is party to, the important people in his or her life, the anxieties of childhood. Elements like these will be constantly reworked as the child's thought matures. The child will ceaselessly search for meaning in life and will retrospectively flesh out the past in accordance with the interpretive models built up in the course of his or her development. Children of two explain what happens to them quite differently than children of four or six. After puberty, a new way of seeing the self emerges, influenced by new opportunities to express sexuality.

In this way the individual continually alters the play of causes that predetermine him. Each memory takes on a new dimension at the different phases in life. Memory is not a storehouse where experiences are piled up without classification. Memory is active, allowing the individual to lend new meanings to the past. It is thanks to this possibility for retroactive reshaping of childhood experience that every person has the opportunity to transform his or her own past through psychotherapy or analysis.

Creative Outcomes

People are continually asking me to predict the futures of very young children. My replies are always very measured, and usually I say as little as possible. Predictions are dangerous, first because they risk sticking to the child and turning into self-fulfilling prophecies, second because they fail to take into account the potential we all have for turning fate around for ourselves.

What I prefer to do in my consultations is to produce a kind of map of the forces involved. What are the parents projecting and anticipating? How are the interactions set up? What is the child's own contribution?

These are parameters that allow us, at best, to imagine the force field that is operating. Beyond that, the best predictive clues are provided by the ability of both parents and child to assimilate new interpretations and reorganize their psychic functioning.

Even if predictions are dangerous, and even if each individual will revise and correct the first edition of his or her destiny, it remains true that each destiny seems to have a central theme.

Mother-baby therapy has established that, from the first months of a child's life, a characteristic theme is spun, upon which the child will progressively design a self-image. Each one of us is able to define what matters most to us, what we hate above all, what we fear, what we hope for. This definition of the "I" is based on unconscious fantasies that sum up fundamental desires, modes of being, relationships with others and with one's own body. This theme is the outcome of a child's natural disposition as well as of the scenarios played out with parents. And the plot of this scenario, as we have seen, is woven by the parents relations with their own ancestors.

This characteristic theme will soon make each baby someone unlike any other. Around this central core, we each, slowly but surely, spin our story and find an identity. At the same time, our earliest encounters with our parents will have a decisive impact on the choices we make, the happiness we know, the setbacks we suffer, throughout life.

A Psychiatry of Hope

❦

*H*uman fate can be conceived as a thick braid in which the strands represent the continuing reemergence of different influences. In this book I have tried to give an account of one of those influences: the early relationships between parent and child and the way these lay down a theme of personal identity.

Other influences will shape a life: heredity, physical makeup, gender, one's mental capacity to organize experience—all these will form part of the braid. Subsequent events will play their part, as will chance occurrences and fateful meetings. Some of these influences are so strong that one can accept them only with resignation and try to adapt. The "red threads" that I have followed here, however—the lasting effect of the primal scenarios linking parents and children for better and for worse—are not fixed. We have seen these scripts change.

Practicing psychiatry is not always fun. All too

often we are consulted too late, when modes of being have been firmly fixed. Then the work consists in resurrecting the past, which takes years, or in reducing the impact of mental suffering upon everyday living. Often people are very slow to realize that some psychic conflict is at the root of their unhappy behavior. It is only after the fact that they understand that their future is bound up with their past and that by throwing some light on what has happened they can improve the chances for things to come. How many years have already been wasted in repeating the same misunderstandings over and over!

When adults in distress confide their histories to me, I always seek to identify the influence of those early scenarios in which parents bond with children. In this way I try to uncover the beginnings of the central themes that guide their destinies. When, in psychoanalytic sessions, I can successfully help patients become aware of the burdensome role that their parents had laid upon them as children, I am always amazed to see how helpful this insight is in showing them the truth of their own past. Generally, patients then notice the huge efforts they have made to fit in with their parents' ideals and to respect their taboos. The realization dawns that the patients had always been moved by some force that came from elsewhere: the constraints and desires of parents had narrowed their field of choice. Once this influence is acknowledged, patients are able to define the constant—and silent because unconscious—presence of this alien force that had hitherto exercised total authority over their destinies. A sense of liberation follows and patients are able once again to feel in charge of their own lives.

In adult psychotherapy, as I listen to the life histories of people who have been powerless prisoners of fate, I have often wondered whether psychotherapy of mother and baby could possibly have changed the course of pathological developments that seemed inevitable.

Certainly there are too many imponderables in the development of any one individual for it to be possible to reply with a categorical yes. Nonetheless, my experience as a practitioner of psychotherapy for very young children has convinced me that early intervention can have a powerful corrective effect on deviations in a child's relationships during the first two years of life.

A relationship that might have taken the form of constant quarreling, perpetual mutual deception, or repetitive misunderstandings changes tone completely once the mechanism of the interaction has been brought into the open. Evelyn Martin and Marie might have continued to live, year in and year out, in an atmosphere of reproach, demand, and avoidance if the influence of an earlier quarrel, between mother and grandmother, had not been made explicit and thus harmless.

As we have seen in the examples I have reported, there is in the period following a child's birth amazing potential for new understanding and hence for radical change. This phase in life is characterized by turmoil, by the resurgence of buried experience, by questioning. Such mental upheaval gives renewed flexibility to old routines and fixed assumptions. This period is more favorable to change than any other phase in life. We should make the most of this potential and support new parents in creative introspection. In this way the spells cast by family ghosts can often be broken so that the child's own nature can be expressed.

Work with parents and infants offers the prospect of a psychiatry of hope, a situation in which, instead of repairing the accumulated misunderstandings of long years, we can work to prevent vicious cycles between parents and children from becoming irreversible. We can forestall misery and crises instead of running to pick up the pieces.

Every parent is influenced by the forces that presided over the formation of his or her family history, for better or for worse. Our ideals, talents, choices of partners or professions, our sweetest dreams as well as darkest depressions are all the product of this long chain of scripts and encounters. Our history recedes into prehistory. Yet each of us has the opportunity to trace back the influences that have led us from an infant's babbling to an adult's decisions—always a rewarding and astonishing journey.

Bibliography

Bowlby, J. *Attachment and Loss*. Vol. I, *Attachment*. New York: Basic Books, 1969.

Brazelton, T. B. *On Becoming a Family*. New York: Delacorte Press/Lawrence, 1981.

Brazelton, T. B., and H. Als. "Four Stages in the Development of Mother-Infant Interaction." In *The Psychoanalytic Study of the Child*, edited by A. Solnit, et al., vol. 34, 1979.

Brazelton, T. B., and B. G. Cramer. *The Earliest Relationship*. Reading, Mass.: Addison-Wesley/Lawrence, 1990.

Cramer, B. G. "Assessment of Parent-Infant Relationships." In *Affective Development in Infancy*, edited by T. B. Brazelton and M. W. Yogman. Norwood, N.J.: Ablex Publishing, 1986.

Cramer, B. G. "Objective and Subjective Aspects of Parent-Infant Relations: An Attempt at Correlation Between Infant Studies and Clinical Work." In *Handbook of Infant Development*, 2d ed., edited by J. Osofsky. New York: John Wiley, 1987.

Cramer, B. G., et al. "Outcome Evaluation in Brief Mother-Infant Psychotherapy." *Infant Mental Health Journal* 11:278–300 (1990).

Bibliography

Cramer, B. G., and D. Stern. "Evaluation of Changes in Mother-Infant Brief Psychotherapy." *Infant Mental Health Journal* 9:1 (Spring 1988).

Emde, R. N., and J. E. Sorce. "The Rewards of Infancy: Emotional Availability and Maternal Referencing." In *Frontiers of Infant Psychiatry*, vol. 2, edited by J. Call, E. Galenson, and R. Tyson. New York: Basic Books, 1983.

Fraiberg, S. *Clinical Studies in Infant Mental Health: The First Year of Life*. London: Tavistock, 1980.

Lebovici, S. *Le Nourisson, La Mère et le Psychanalyste*. Paris: Editions Le Centurion, 1983.

Mahler, M. *On Human Symbiosis and the Vicissitudes of Individuation*. Vol. I, *Infantile Psychosis*. New York: International Universities Press, 1968.

Mahler, M. S., F. Pine, and A. Bergman. *The Psychological Birth of the Human Infant*. New York: Basic Books, 1975.

Stern, D. *The Interpersonal World of the Infant*. New York: Basic Books, 1985.

Winnicott, D. W. "The Newborn and His Mother." In *Babies and Their Mothers*, edited by C. Winnicott, R. Shepherd, and M. Davis. Reading, Mass.: Addison-Wesley/Lawrence, 1987.

Winnicott, D. W. *The Child, the Family, and the Outside World*. London: Penguin, 1964. Reading, Mass.: Addison-Wesley/Lawrence, 1987.

Index

❧

About the Author

Bertrand G. Cramer, M.D., is Professor of Child Psychiatry at the University of Geneva and a practicing psychoanalyst. He is a pioneer in infant psychiatry and trains doctors, psychologists, and nurses in this field. Dr. Cramer is Vice President of the World Association for Infant Psychiatry and Allied Disciplines. A graduate of the New York Psychoanalytic Institute, he has trained elsewhere in the United States and in Europe. In 1982–1983, he was Visiting Professor at Harvard Medical School. In addition to over seventy scholarly papers, Dr. Cramer is the author of *Psychiatrie du Bébé* and coauthor, with T. Berry Brazelton, M.D., of *The Earliest Relationship*.

About the Translator

Gillian Gill, writer and translator, is the author of *Agatha Christie: The Woman and Her Mysteries* and the translator of many works of psychiatry and psychoanalysis.